Sebastopol
to Dagenham

Sebastopol to Dagenham

Crimean War Letters
of
Captain Thomas Basil Fanshawe
33rd (Duke of Wellington's) Regiment

Transcribed by Deirdre Marculescu
Edited by Derek Alexander
& Matt Benjamin

Valence House Publications

Published in 2016 by Valence House Publications
Valence House, Becontree Avenue
Dagenham, Essex RM8 3HT

www.valencehousecollections.co.uk

ISBN 978-1-911391-02-9

Front Cover Image : 'Looking towards Mackenzie's
Heights, tents of the 33rd Regiment in the foreground'
Roger Fenton (1855)
Library of Congress, reference LC-USZC4-9272

Back Cover Image : Crimean War Medal awarded to
Captain TB Fanshawe 1855 (LBBD Archives, Valence House)

Cover : Trevor Wilson Design

Thomas Basil Fanshawe (1829 - 1905)

By Mrs Carpenter (1857)

Valence House Museum

These letters were written from the Crimea by

Thomas Basil Fanshawe

2nd son of the Rev. Thomas Lewis Fanshawe

of Parsloes Dagenham, Essex

He served the whole of his Military Career

in the 33rd Duke of Wellingtons Regiment

which included the Crimea, the Indian Mutiny

and the Abyssinian Campaign.

He eventually commanded the Regiment.

He obtained his first commission 14th April 1846,

became Captain [in 1854], Major in 1864,

Lt. Col 24th Sept 1873 and retired with the

Honorary rank of Colonel 2nd March 1878.

He was born 3rd Dec 1829

married 8th March 1864

Emily Catherine, youngest daughter of

Gerard Lipyeatt Gosselin of

Mount Ospringe, Kent

and died 4th May 1905

(Reproduced from the frontispiece of the bound
volume containing the original letters)

Thomas Basil Fanshawe and his family at Dagenham Vicarage

Captain Thomas Basil Fanshawe was well educated, socially confident and outwardly sophisticated – typical characteristics of many young officers serving in British regiments during the 19th century. Yet through his personal letters Basil (as he was known) reveals an engaging personality that deserves our attention.

Aged in his mid-twenties during his service in Crimea, he shows a character that is a charming mix of youthful curiosity and considerable responsible maturity. Despite the 160 years that have passed since the Crimean War, and changes in styles and manners, Basil remains easy to like. He was a sociable fellow, and his 'clubbable' personality easily bridges the years.

First impressions are usually revised, of course, and with knowledge of his family life and a degree of empathy the reader can be absorbed by the subtleties of Basil's style and language. He adapts these slightly according to who he is writing to, but his narrative is always clear and straightforward, making it simple to align with his world.

The interests and pursuits that he shared with his family tied them together and their letters are full of everyday life in their neighbourhood, and the updating of personal and national news.

Basil's mother was his most avid correspondent and his relationship with her is very strong. She supplied him with reassurance and confirmation of his value, even though for nine years he had lived an army life and was resourceful, mature and independent.

His father, Thomas Lewis Fanshawe, the vicar of Dagenham, was in his early sixties and not in robust health. Basil tried to disturb him the least, generally limiting his comments to the regiment or to their mutual love of shooting on the Dagenham marshes. As they passed back and forth details of game seen and shot in Crimea and on the marshes, they found their way of staying in touch.

John Gaspard Fanshawe, Basil's elder brother, received his more frank confidences concerning the situation in Crimea. These often communicate details of high ranking officers, leaving us to assume that little or no censorship applied during the Crimean War. John Gaspard had a career in the Parliamentary service at Westminster. The brothers' dialogue echoes that of the common-room, London club or officer's mess. They enjoy sharing news of mutual friends and acquaintances - invariably referred to by surname only.

Basil appears less comfortable with his brother-in-law, Edward 'Den' Denison, a barrister fifteen years his senior. Maybe his wary deference is understandable.

By contrast, Basil's recently married sister-in-law 'Bab' was very close to his own age, and he seems to have found in her a new good friend. He writes to her about her young son and enjoys her news of the goings-on of daily life. He kept reserved for his own older sister, Helen, that familiar attitude generally bestowed by brotherly affection.

For his younger brother Dick, undisciplined and free, Basil enjoyed expressing an exasperated tolerance, although they were obviously great pals.

In common with all families, the Fanshawes had been shaped by their history, which was well documented. Their earliest ancestors came from Fanshawe Gate in Derbyshire. Descendants arrived in Dagenham and nearby Barking during the Elizabethan period, and soon became the principal landowners in the area. When Basil's father succeeded to the estate of Parsloes Manor with its great tracts of local land and property, he was the latest in an unbroken line that had descended from father to son for 300 years.

The first to settle in the area was Henry Fanshawe, the Queen's Remembrancer of the Exchequer. In 1555 he married a widow with property in Barking and soon after purchased the Manors of Jenkins and Valence (Valence House[1]) and other lands. On his death, the reversion of the post of Remembrancer and most of his estate was passed to his nephew and protégé, Thomas Fanshawe.

Appointing the sheriffs and overseeing tax revenues, Thomas Fanshawe came to be one of Queen Elizabeth's most trusted and loyal courtiers. He greatly increased the family's position and wealth by diligence and planning. He purchased a large estate at Ware Park on the Great North Road and through his two marriages, and those of his sons and daughters, the family became connected to many powerful families in the Tudor Court, including Mildmay, Cecil, Bourchier, Walsingham, Smythe, and Hatton.

Thomas Fanshawe provided for all his three sons when he died. They were well positioned in the Stuart court, firstly close to the ill-fated Henry, Prince of Wales and after his death, to his younger brother Prince Charles, later King Charles I.

At the outbreak of the Civil War in 1642, the family declared their loyalty as Royalists, joining King Charles in the exiled court at Oxford. When the King fled to the North he entrusted Sir Richard Fanshawe to take his son, the 14 year old Prince of Wales, to safe exile. They made escape by a perilous route across the West of England, eventually sailing to the Channel Isles and then on to France.

Later, following the Battle of Worcester in 1651, Sir Richard was captured and spent seven years under house arrest. After Cromwell's death he was able to escape to France and join King Charles II. In 1660 he was on the King's ship returning to England for Restoration.

Appointed Latin Secretary to the King, he travelled to Portugal and negotiated and completed the contract for the King's marriage to Catherine of Braganza. Soon afterwards he became Ambassador to Portugal and Spain.

---

[1] Valence House Museum situated in Valence Park, Dagenham

Another grandson of Thomas Fanshawe, Sir Thomas Fanshawe of Jenkins, remained settled at Jenkins[1], the manor that spanned the border between Dagenham and Barking. This branch of the family were also Royalist and held high office as Surveyor General and other senior legal positions.

William, the third son of Thomas Fanshawe, purchased the Manor of Parsloes[2] in 1619. This property eventually passed down to Basil's father, Thomas Lewis Fanshawe, and is frequently mentioned in Basil's letters which often express concern for its future.

By the early 18th century, the families at Ware Park and at Jenkins had died out through the male line, but generations of daughters had married into other important families. However, some had married men from other Fanshawe lines, and as a consequence Basil was descended from all three sons of Thomas Fanshawe.

The family's fortunes had changed much since 1601 when the wealthy Thomas Fanshawe had planned a future for his sons and daughters. The values of honour and loyalty expressed in his will survived, and the family's reputation remained in high esteem. But how could Thomas have anticipated the Civil War and the harsh monetary penalty that would be exacted from his descendants for their royal allegiance? Eventually his great estate at Ware Park would be sold to repay Civil War debts.

In later years the Fanshawes adopted new careers. In the remodelled Navy, members of the family rose to the rank of Vice-Admiral and Admiral, and in the Army they were equally successful. Others entered the legal professions and the Church, and in the 19th century they joined the burgeoning civil and colonial service. Some had outstanding artistic and literary talents, in particular the poet and artist Catherine Maria Fanshawe (1765-1834) and the author Althea Fanshawe (1759-1824).

---

[1] The site of Jenkins - the land now occupied by Mayesbrook Park, Barking.
[2] The site of Parsloes – the land now occupied by Parsloes Park, Dagenham.

Sons and daughters continued to marry well, often linking the family to great merchants of the City and sometimes names such as Gascoyne and Gaspard were added to Fanshawe recognising connections.

The sons of the family at Parsloes attended public school. Thomas Lewis Fanshawe and his eldest son went to Eton, and the two younger sons Basil and Dick travelled further afield to Shrewsbury. In those establishments they began to form their own circles of contacts and connections, and the names of their school colleagues are traceable through Basil's letters.

Life on a gentleman's country estate at Parsloes could be peaceful with traditional country pursuits and long walks in the fresh air, but London's lively social scene was close at hand.

All this Basil took away with him as he left home at sixteen to join the 33rd Regiment, nearly ten years before the outbreak of the Crimean War. Even then he had an air of confidence based upon his family's social standing and honourable reputation, giving him the sense of pride and assurance conveyed in his letters. At home he had been constantly surrounded by the evidence of 'his' history, as portraits[1] of generations of his ancestors hung on the walls of Dagenham Vicarage and Parsloes Manor.

Despite Basil's air of confidence he never lacks care for others and his letters show a concern for the welfare of most of his brother officers. His more impatient and dismissive remarks are usually reserved for officers he considers to be lazy or lacking integrity. A sense of fair play seems to have been deeply important to Basil…

The letters contain little information about non-commissioned men, so we should take notice of the few occasions he mentions

---

[1] Valence House Museum, Dagenham was gifted a part of the Fanshawe family collection in 1963: 49 paintings, with a further 7 received in 2004. This collection, considered of national importance, is almost unique as a family collection from the late Tudor and Stuart periods. Artists include Marcus Gheeraerts the Younger, William Dobson, Peter Lely, Mary Beale and other known court painters.

unnamed men of his company. He speaks of 'uneducated men' not in a belittling way but with understanding, appreciating their situation and encouraging improvements to their lives. His constant requests for copies of the *Illustrated London News* it is to be noted, were not for himself, but for the men.

Captain Fanshawe was clearly ambitious. The military achievements of his mother's family, the Le Marchants, must have created a competitiveness between him and his many first cousins. Like him, many achieved higher rank.

Basil's mother, Catherine Le Marchant, was from Guernsey in the Channel Islands, the eldest daughter of Major General John Gaspard Le Marchant whose own army career had been outstanding.

As a young officer, observing that British equipment was out of date, Le Marchant had redesigned the sabre and written a manual of sabre exercises. His methods were so successful they were adopted for general use by all the regiments. He also became increasingly concerned that the practice of purchasing commissions meant that formal training and development of British officers was almost non-existent. He sought the patronage of King George III to initiate the first training school for officers, the Royal Military Academy at High Wycombe. Not only did he set up the college, but was also appointed its first superintendent. It soon proved highly successful and Le Marchant was promoted to the rank of Major General.

In 1811 he was despatched to command the Heavy Cavalry Brigade in Wellington's army during the Peninsular War. Back at High Wycombe, tragedy struck when his wife Mary died in childbirth leaving a family of ten children. The eldest daughter, Catherine, only 14 when her mother died, became her father's primary correspondent and he wrote[1] poignant letters to her from the battlefields. Catherine would later become Basil's mother.

---

[1] Copies of the letters written by Major General John Gaspard Le Marchant addressed to his daughter {K}atherine are retained in the Fanshawe Collection at Valence House, Dagenham (fully transcribed).

Descendant Chart for sons of John Gaspard Le Marchant

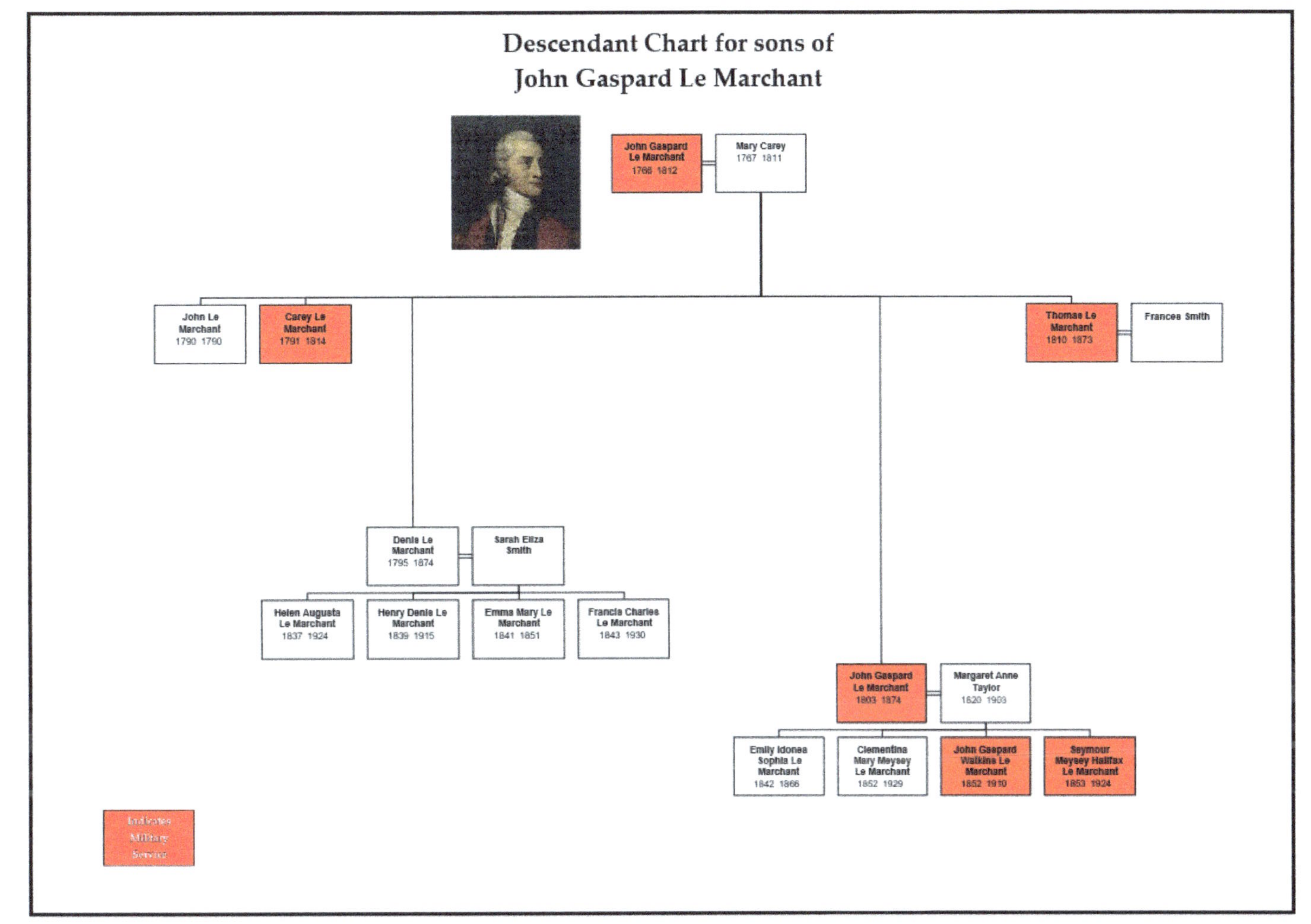

Descendant Chart for daughters of
John Gaspard Le Marchant

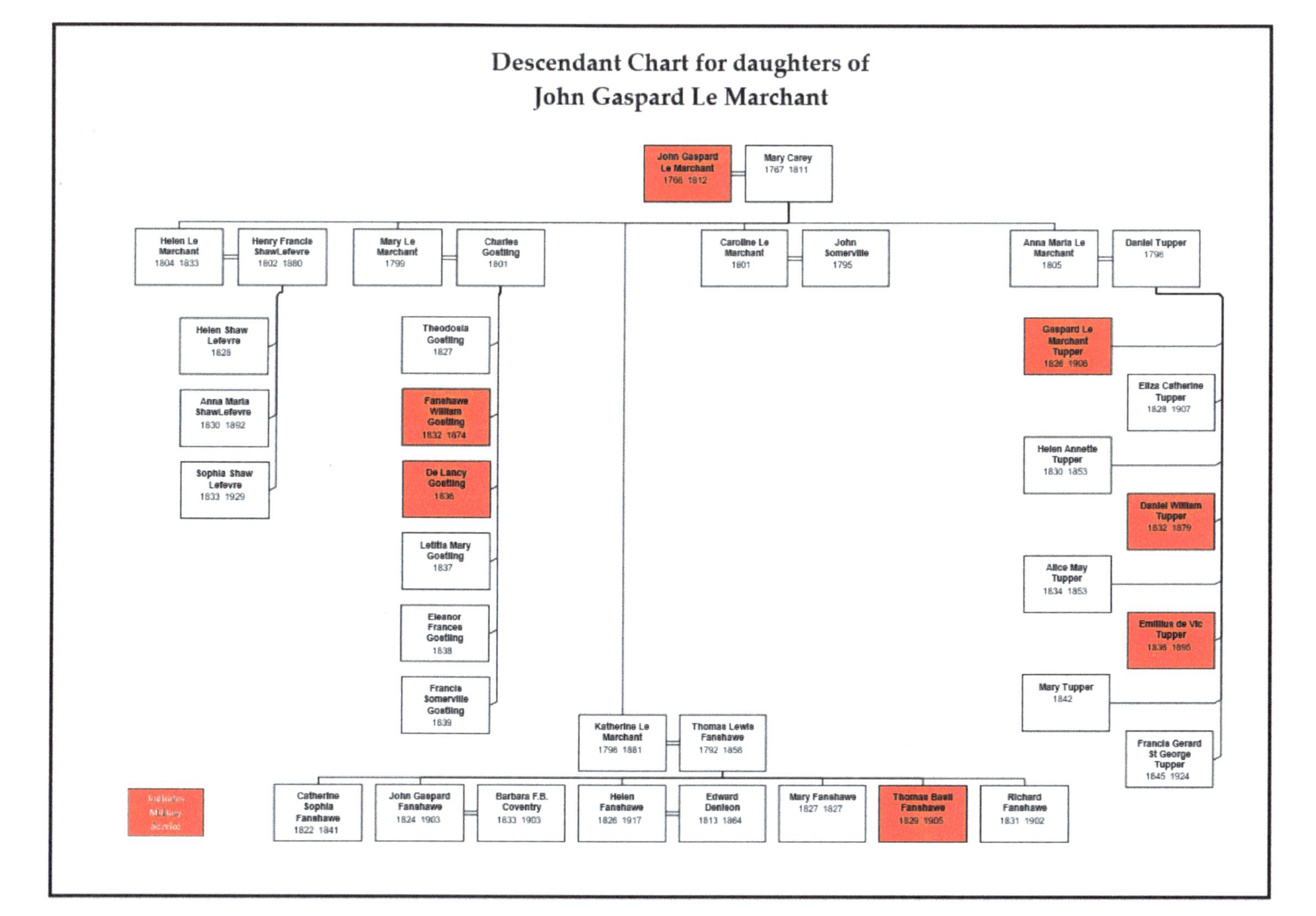

On Wellington's direct orders, Le Marchant led a decisive cavalry charge against the French Army at Salamanca in July 1812. Strategically he was brilliantly successful and put the French to rout, but tragically was killed by a stray shot during the final moments of the action. He was buried on the battlefield at Salamanca.

The victory was such that Major General Le Marchant became a national hero and a memorial to him was erected in St Paul's Cathedral. Parliament raised a substantial pension for the support of his orphaned children.

Carey Le Marchant, the eldest son and Aide de Camp to his father, survived the Battle of Salamanca but died in action two years later. The next son, Denis, was still schoolboy at Eton and remained there sharing his room and his sorrow with Thomas Lewis Fanshawe. It was another ten years before they became brothers-in-law…

Catherine Le Marchant left her school for gentlemen's daughters in Marlow and returned to Guernsey with her four sisters and younger brothers to be raised by their extended family. Later, one of the younger brothers would enlist in the army, and Catherine and her married sisters encouraged their own sons to join the regiments in keeping with family tradition.

Basil's letters reveal the close links between all the Le Marchant families. He had no Fanshawe first cousins, so his wider family were exclusively the relatives of his mother. Through his letters we hear of his parents' visits to Guernsey and his aunts and uncles' travels and family meetings. His letters, with the Christian names (and sometimes shortened familiar names) of his Guernsey aunts, uncles and cousins reveal how many of his first cousins were serving in different regiments in the Crimea.

The work and life of Basil's grandfather, Major General John Gaspard Le Marchant is today still commemorated at Sandhurst, the modern Royal Military Academy, where his portrait hangs in the room that bears his name.

His must surely have been a powerful and inspiring legacy for Basil and his cousins as they grew up 25 or more years after his death.

All these facts are peripheral to the view which Basil Fanshawe gives us of the Crimean War, for his letters may easily be read and appreciated without additional information. As private letters, however, they deserve to be read in more than one dimension. Clearly he wrote only for those that already understood him. If we enter his space with interest and care, we will be able to accept his comments in the spirit in which they were made.

How sad that we have no record of the replies from his family ...

Dagenham Village

The parish of Dagenham, twelve miles east of the City of London, was bounded by the River Thames to the south, and the ancient forest of Hainault to the north. This landscape attracted 7th century Saxons to establish Daeccanham (meaning Daecca's homestead), one of their earliest recorded settlements in Essex.

Moving forward to the era in which these letters were written, the population of Dagenham had only reached 2,494 at the time of the 1851 census. Further up river, London was vastly expanding in all directions, but little disturbed the rhythm of Dagenham's rural life.

Landowners and farmers of the parish may have become well established and prosperous, but most local people still laboured on the land as they had done for centuries, or plied their trades in small businesses. At work and play the villagers lived in a neighbourhood where everyone knew everyone else, and many were related by a web of marriages over several generations.

Generations of families grew their seasonal crops, raised their livestock and bought and sold at the market in the nearby country town of Romford, less than three miles away.

The parish church of St. Peter & St. Paul, first recorded in 1205 and greatly enlarged since, stood at the heart of Dagenham Village. Its vicar, the Reverend Thomas Lewis Fanshawe, had competition for the souls of the parish when dissenting chapels became established. Methodism attracted a strong following in the village. A Wesleyan chapel in Bull Street opened in 1846 and the Ecclesiastical Census of 1851 shows 264 worshippers.

A Dagenham farmer named William Ford had bequeathed £10,000 to establish a free school and Basil's father the Reverend Thomas Lewis Fanshawe had also opened a small infant school near the church.

The Metropolitan Police arrived in Dagenham in 1840. In 1846 the unsolved murder of 20 year-old village policeman George Clark embroiled the local force and residents in a scandal that shocked the nation. This notoriety was only brief and Dagenham soon slipped back into peaceful obscurity.

Close proximity to London and the Thames inevitably brought change with new inventions for industries and transport. A failed project of 1846 attempted to link the Dagenham riverside with the Eastern Counties Railway line passing through Chadwell Heath. In 1854 Sir John Rennie mooted another scheme to link Dagenham Breach to the Thames via a lock, and also to the branch of the London, Tilbury and Southend Railway newly extended east from Barking. This was also unsuccessful, but his idea pointed in the right direction, and nearly thirty years later Samuel Williams accomplished the link. He went on to establish his large shipbuilding, civil engineering and transport business which proved to be the catalyst for the industrial prosperity in south Essex during the next century.

In 1855 all that was a long way off and Basil's father, the principal landowner of the area, was still able to enjoy the countryside surrounding Dagenham Village.

Familiar to Fanshawes were the fields and working farms occupied by other families whose names appear as often as their own in the parish registers and vestry minutes. Relevant are the references made by Basil and his brother Dick concerning changes taking place in the village during their absence. Although these changes may have been relatively minor and trivial, they were important to that small community, and research into Dagenham's Vestry minutes confirms discussions taking place on the same issues. Basil's letters throw an unexpected light onto the debates, subtly revealing likely alliances of self-interest and conflicts being resolved outside the formal minuted meetings.

In Basil's day, changes in Dagenham took place slowly. Sixty years later however, after World War I, rapid changes engulfed the village. The area was chosen by the London County Council for its biggest 'Homes fit for heroes' social housing project, the Becontree Estate.

Dagenham Village has now almost disappeared. The lovely old church still stands, as does Basil's home, which in the late 1970s ceased to be used as a vicarage. Now in private hands, it is currently under renovation.

Parsloes Manor became too difficult for the family to maintain and in the early 20th century it was sold by Basil's nephew Evelyn. It was demolished by the London County Council in 1925 and all that remains is the surrounding parkland, now Parsloes Park, one of Dagenham's beautiful green spaces.

However, the LCC meticulously researched the area's history when the estate was being constructed, and many of its new roads were given names associated with the Fanshawe family. Each day when residents move about the streets the Fanshawe names are constantly mentioned, unwittingly or not – confirmation of the family's relevance to contemporary local life, even after 400 years.

The British involvement in the Crimean War 1854 – 1856

In the rapidly expanding industrial age of early Victorian England, prosperity had resulted from forty years of peace. Conflict had been avoided in Europe by carefully negotiated diplomacy, choreographed by the great powers of France, Russia and Britain, each anxious to protect their own trade interests and access to free movement of shipping.

Conflict eventually spilled over when Russia, anticipating the decline of the ancient Ottoman Empire, made expansive moves into regions around the Black Sea that had traditionally been occupied by the Turks.

The flashpoint came when the French re-opened their long standing dispute with Russia concerning the question of rights to control the keys to Christian holy places in the Middle East. The French, traditionally empowered to act in the interests of all Roman Catholics, disputed Russia's demands as they attempted to exercise their own privilege and obligation to keep safe all eastern Orthodox Christians under the Sultan's rule.

Britain weighed in, and choosing to support the Turks with the French, declared war on Russia on March 28th 1854.

Allied troops landed on the Crimean Peninsula in southern Russia in September 1854, joining Turks and Sardinians. On 20th of that month they engaged in a major battle at Alma on north shore opposite the fortified port of Sebastopol which was their objective. A total of 36,000 men of all sides fought and over 5,000 were killed or wounded.

On 25th October the fight moved south to the lesser port of Balaclava where the British were now on the defensive. The first line of Turks were soon overcome and the British troops became heavily engaged yet the 'Thin Red Line' held and they beat the Russians back.

At Balaclava, Britain's Heavy Brigade successfully charged and defeated almost all of the enemy cavalry, but ironically the ill-conceived Charge of the Light Brigade today remains at the forefront of the nation's memory of Balaclava, and indeed the whole conflict.

Eleven days later, the action moved north again where the combatants met at Inkerman. This time the Allies numbered less than 16,000 yet faced a Russian army that had swelled to 42,000. Allied casualties numbered nearly 5,000 that day, but the Russian losses were double that number. Despite appalling weather, the Allies held their ground.

Familiar with their own land, the Russians knew the oncoming winter would be on their side. Under the cover of dense fog, they withdrew into Sebastopol's city walls, leaving the Allies to make camp outside.

Inside the heavy fortifications of their old city, behind a secure harbour inlet and well protected by sunken ships across the outer harbour, the Russians had time to build their defences. They knew winter conditions would soon take a heavy toll on the camps that surrounded their besieged city.

Extremely harsh winter weather overwhelmed the British. They were neither battle-hardened nor well-equipped, and soon disease was rife due to inadequate sanitation. The French fared a little better, as their shelters were more substantial than the British tents.

Back in England, the poor planning and preparation for the conflict was becoming a major political issue. The general public were alerted through news received by telegraph and reported in *The Times*. In January 1855 a large crowd mounted the so-called Snowball Riot in Trafalgar Square to make their protest.

Parliament was in uproar and the government of Lord Aberdeen was brought down. The new Prime Minister, Lord Palmerston, took a determined line and insisted that immediate improvements were necessary if Crimea was not to become a total disaster. Equipment, especially shelters, was to be despatched. To resolve the crisis in the health of the troops, new methods of nursing were commissioned. Additional troops were mustered and re-enforcing units were soon ready for embarkation.

By the late spring of 1855, troop ships were bound for the Crimea, full of fresh young soldiers. Included among them was Captain Thomas Basil Fanshawe, and his letters take up the story from this point on. His view is not from memory, but written in the heat of the moment. We will soon be travelling with him somewhere between Dagenham and Sebastopol…

Bull Inn & Post Office – in Bull Lane, Dagenham c.1900

LBBD Archives at Valence House

The Journey of the Letters

Thomas Basil Fanshawe, a Captain in the 33rd (Duke of Wellington's) Regiment, wrote to his mother on 13th June 1855. He was travelling through the eastern Mediterranean on the troop ship SS Andes, bound for the Crimea in southern Russia. A few months short of his twenty-sixth birthday, he had served in the regiment for nearly ten years, enjoying his life of travel and adventure in the familiar company of his brother officers. He was ambitious for promotion for himself, but also cared for and encouraged his men through the daily routines essential to army discipline.

Known as Basil by his family, he was the second of three boys and had a natural, thoughtful and optimistic personality. His early independence had given him the maturity to appreciate his present picturesque journey but at the same time he understood it was a prelude to a campaign certain to be vastly different from his previous experience. He knew his outcome could not be certain or assured.

His mother, Catherine, comfortably at home in the Vicarage at Dagenham, was always his closest correspondent. It was her glorious stories of her father Major General John Gaspard Le Marchant that had inspired him in youth to an army career. Now she delighted in his own regimental exploits, but any pride she had in his achievements and ambitions was tempered with an understanding of how soldiers' loyalties were pulled between family, home and the army.

Basil relied on his mother to remind the family to write regularly with news from home and she replied to his first letter by return of post. Soon letters from his father, brothers and sister followed.

Every letter his mother received was passed on to her other children, keeping them up to date with life in Sebastopol. With her encouragement, they circulated their letters. Eventually she gathered all the letters together and made copies in her own hand of those not been addressed to her. The result is this complete collection of Basil's Crimean War correspondence.

The letters show the family at Dagenham Vicarage to be warm and caring. The same gentle affection was also extended to the many aunts, uncles and cousins on the Le Marchant side of Basil's family, and it is evident that the whole group shared mutual interests.

Today, through these unsentimental letters we can discover a way of life not vastly different from our own. Their language is surprisingly modern, with many familiar words and idiomatic phrases that help us slip easily into their circle and focus on the Crimean battlefield.

Let's now visualise the arrival of Basil's first letter.

In common with the rest of Europe, Dagenham had experienced exceptionally harsh weather throughout the first half of 1855. People were well aware that in the Crimea the soldiers, sheltering only in tents, had suffered badly, particularly the British. A large number had succumbed to the freezing conditions and many more died of cholera and dysentery.

Basil had been fortunate in that he arrived in the Crimea after that terrible winter and the first battles at Alma, Balaclava[1] and Inkerman. Reaching Sebastopol he found the Russians well dug in and prepared for a long siege from inside the city's massive fortification, the Great Redan.

Basil's first letter arrived in Dagenham around Midsummer Day when it was brought down from London by rail to Romford. The station had only been opened sixteen years, but the system was well established that young Kettle, Dagenham's teenage post runner,

---

[1] Balaclava – spelling varies in the letters between Balaclava and Balaklava.

collected the post and carried it the three miles to the Dagenham village post office at the Bull Inn.

In 1855 the postal service was something of a family concern at Dagenham, for the Postmaster was George Kettle (or Kittle), the Bull's landlord. His duties required signing for and checking two deliveries of incoming mail and one despatch daily, which he presumably organised around his main occupation.

Letters bound for Dagenham most likely were addressed to only a few families, and mostly for the Reverend Thomas Lewis Fanshawe, his wife and family. Naturally, parish matters would be included in his post, but he was also the owner of Parsloes Manor, and must have received considerable estate correspondence and business papers. There would have been a healthy amount of social correspondence too.

The postmaster might have been curious about many Fanshawe letters but surely he would have been interested to see Basil's first letter pass through his hands. He too had a relative on active service in the Crimea, as we know from Basil's letters in which he refers to a visit from a soldier he calls 'Kettle'. Basil mentions seeing 'Kettle' in camp at Sebastopol and he appears to be responding to an enquiry. The two soldiers' conversation appears amiable and comfortable despite their difference of rank. If we assume different levels of society mixed in Dagenham's public houses, churches and civic meetings, there is every reason to suppose that the two had shared previous conversation. Home on leave, Basil surely must have taken the three minute walk from the Vicarage to the Bull to enjoy a pint or two…

Basil's 'Dearest Mother' cherished his letters and they were bound, probably by her eldest son, John Gaspard Fanshawe, who placed them in his library with his bookplate in the cover. His extensive library at Parsloes Manor and at his London residence in Halkin Street West contained many antiquarian books and family papers, and during his life he gradually distributed them between his children. Any remaining books were similarly shared after his death.

The Crimea letters were given to Violet, his younger daughter, who married the Honourable Huntly Gordon. A more recent custodian has been their grandson, John Gordon, who was well aware of his great-great uncle's army career and the interest the letters might hold for historians. However the handwriting of both Basil and his mother Catherine is challenging, and the letters have not been fully studied for many years.

Newly transcribed for this volume, the letters reveal Basil's youthful personality. He is engaging, and, to use his own words, 'very fresh'. His view of his time and place is so well expressed that he has quite unintentionally woven his own soldier's story into a narrative that needs little embellishment.

We at Valence House are immensely grateful to John Gordon for sharing Basil's story with us. We are in his debt for his interest in our work, his friendship and his generosity. In addition to these letters, he has donated family papers and other material to our Fanshawe collection over many years. This generosity provides unique opportunities for others to rediscover stories of his ancestors who connect to so many other families of Barking and Dagenham past.

In return for his gifts, John requests only our enthusiasm to explore and share the stories we reveal. So it is with thanks that we hereby comply and offer this publication for his and your appreciation.

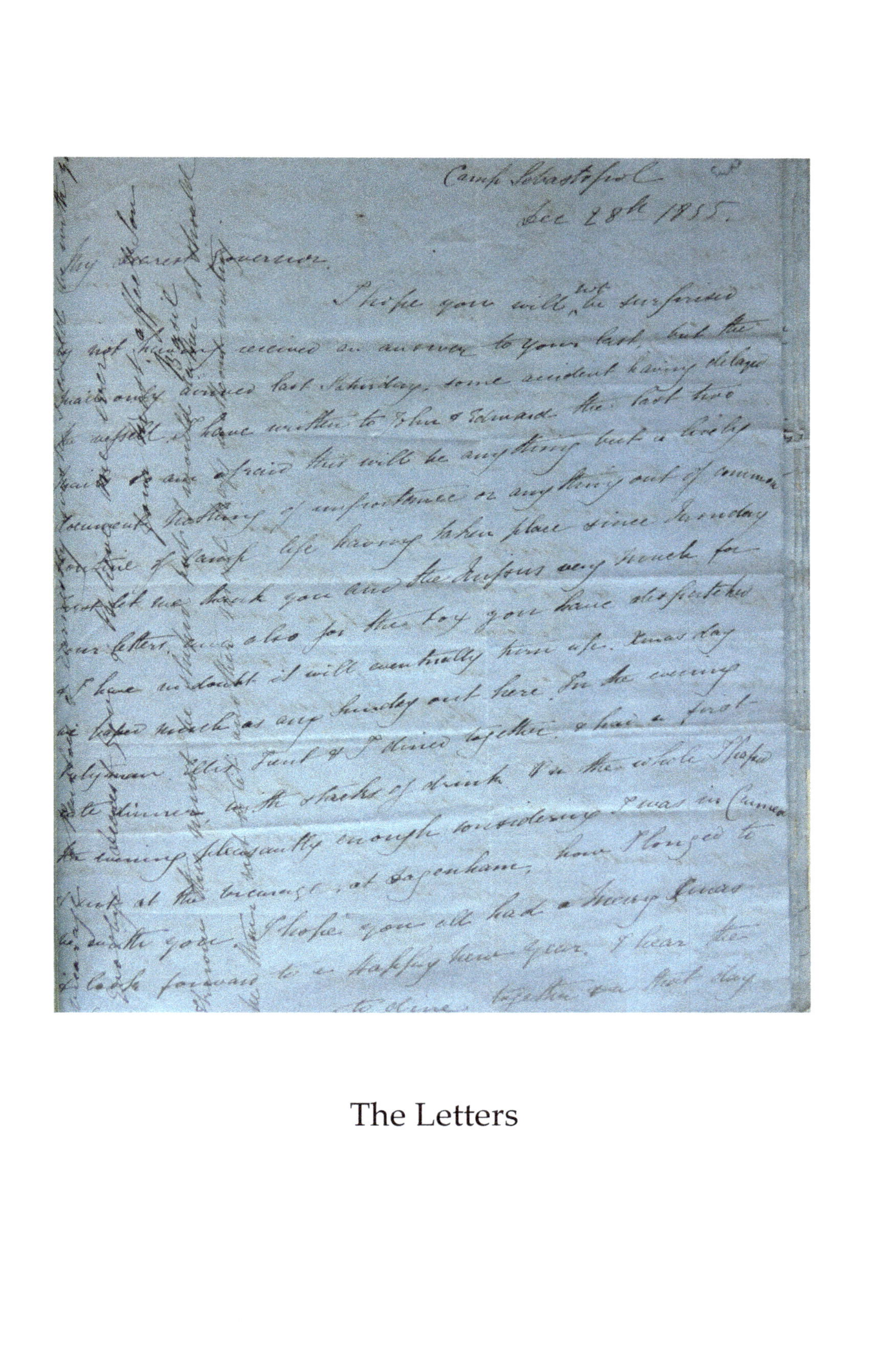

Camp Sebastopol
Dec 28th 1855.

My dearest Governor,

I hope you will not be surprised [...]

The Letters

Transcribers Notes

Capt. Fanshawe's handwriting is relatively easy to read allowing for the semi transparency of the paper. He has written on both sides of each sheet of paper with ink that is not always consistent and he had a need to be economical as postage was prohibitive. As a consequence he made hardly any attempt to punctuate or paragraph his letters to allow more space.

Lack of punctuation creates a problem with the flow of the letters, when read in the original and an early decision was made to insert punctuation in the transcription for ease and enjoyment of the letters.

No other 'improvements' were necessary, as his spelling was almost perfect and he made very few errors that were not self-corrected. As with all good correspondents he wrote with energy and immediacy.

With patience I have transcribed most of his words, but those that elude me are shown by the symbols below.

[ ]   transcriber's addition or comment.
[xxx]   indecipherable word or part word - x relating
                to approximate number of letters.
( )   comments bracketed by TBF in his letters.

Place Names - mostly verified by maps, but within the letters TBF occasionally uses various different spellings for the same place.

Written by Thomas Basil Fanshawe - to his mother, Catherine Fanshawe.
SS 'Andes'
Wednesday June 13th 1855

My dearest Mother

I suppose you will have seen the papers and heard from Aunt Mary that I have left Malta. My last letter will have led you to think of my speedy departure, and they sent us off in a hurry on board this ship instead of the Great Tasmania of which we have decidedly the best, as from all accounts that ship is a most uncomfortable one. We have 820 men on board and some 25 officers of whom I am the senior captain.

We left Malta on Thursday night, taking in tow a ship with mules, the latter held on to us till Monday morning when she broke adrift & it was blowing too hard to come nearer, so we left her to make the best of her way over by herself. We have been very fortunate at present as to our own passage, no one a bit seedy. It came on to blow fresh on Monday, but that was all. After rounding Cape Matapan[1] we have hardly left sight of land but we did not go very close to any of the Islands. The Dardanelles[2] are very fine and a most beautiful looking country, we entered them yesterday morning & got out of them 12 o/c last night. We are now in a thick fog going very slow about an hour from Constantinople. Whether I shall have time to give you an opinion of Constantinople I know not, I am rather afraid not. It is now about ¼ to 8 o/c and as we have to water

---

[1] Cape Matapan – at the southernmost point of mainland Greece, an important place for thousands of years, believed by the ancient Greeks to be the home of Hades the god of the dead. Throughout the centuries, mercenaries gathered at this point to wait for employment.
[2] Connecting the Black Sea to the Mediterranean Sea, the Dardenelles like the Bosphorus separates Europe from the mainland of Asia. It is considered an international waterway.

I suppose we shall not start again for our destination till tomorrow. Balaclava is only 44 hours from Const.

You will be pleased to hear that <u>the</u> box from Tompkins turned up the night before I left Malta. The cheese I delivered to the Gostlings and the Col. told me it was first rate & in capital order. Tomkins sent the box out with a horse belonging to Major Green (68th). I had such a lot to do handing over my company, etc, etc, I could not properly get up to the Gostlings[1] to say goodbye & thank them for their kindness. The Col came on board to see me off & he brought me a most useful compendium in the shape of a pocket book containing everything useful from Eleanor. I have just been writing to them. I packed up all my woollen things which arrived in the box & which I liked best & did not want to take with me in a portmanteau to be sent to the Gostlings so that they could send it on if I require it. The box contained a most useful supply of warm comfortable things.

I have heard no news from the Crimea for an age but you have all the latest intelligence duly reported in The Times I suppose within 24 hours after everything occurs.

After, I shall find I hope, a letter of yours, in the meanwhile I hope I shall find all my old friends of the Regt well on arriving.

PS - Have just arrived at Constantinople & am off in an hour so must close with my best love to you & to the Govr[2] and all at Parsloes, ever dearest mother

Your affectionate son
Basil

---

[1] Mary Le Marchant – sister of TBF's mother, married to Lt. Colonel Charles Gostling stationed in Malta (daughters Eleanor & Geraldine).
[2] Father of TBF – Rev. Thomas Lewis Fanshawe, Vicar of Dagenham and owner of Parsloes Manor, Dagenham.

Written by Thomas Basil Fanshawe - to his mother.
Camp Sebastopol
June 19th 1855

My dearest Mother

I consider myself excessively lucky to be now able to write to you as
I can assure you that I little did picture to do so about 5 or 6 o/c
yesterday morning when under fire. But to begin, I left Malta last
Thursday week and reached Constantinople as I told you in my last
the day I wrote. As we were told we were only to be an hour and a
half on shore, the first thing I did was to post your letter then
walked about the town through the Bazaar & the mosque of St.
Sophia.

The Bazaar is a very rum place, long narrow rows of shops and
really each row special to its particular thing which they sell such as
boots in one row etc. The mosque is a very fine building but I
thought it would have been much more decorated from what I have
heard of eastern magnificence. I have been in a good many Turkish
towns of the lower & worst description but they are all clean to the
Turkish capital, for of all filthy stinking ill travelled places it beats
them out & out.

I then had to go on board & found we did not sail till the next
morning. So I went up to the Golden Horn[1] a long way up in a
barque (I do not know how to spell the name right) & enjoyed it
very much. The Bosphorus is a very pretty sail & takes about 2½
hours to go up, we got to Balaclava on Friday afternoon about 4 o/c,
but did not disembark till Sunday morning, it is a long hot march up

---

[1] Golden Horn – the 'horn' shaped natural harbour dividing the old city of
Constantinople from the more modern. The city's great trading reputation and or
the bright reflecting golden light at sunset could account for its description.

to Camp. Leaving Balaclava about 11 we did not arrive in Camp till 4.

The same night I was the only one of the draft ordered up with the Regt which with the whole brigade of our Division was to support an attack on the Redan[1]. The French at the same time took the round tower. The whole thing whatever the papers may say, was frightfully mismanaged. We had about 150 yards of open ground to cross & exposed to Russian fire of grape as thick & fast as they could send it. How I escaped being bowled over is a wonder.

We lost 50 men, killed & wounded. Lt. Colonel Johnstone[2] lost his left arm. Mundy[3] hit in the leg with a bullet, Collings[4] got hit by something but only stunned for a moment. Bennett[5] was killed, Heyland[6] missing, Quayle[7] shot in the arm & elbow but I hope will get it right. Wickham[8], hit in the foot & likely to be a long job. I got a bruise on the shoulder from either a stone or a grape shell, but I fancy the former. My arm was a little stiff yesterday but that was all. The rest of our fellows got off all right. I got home with the rest of our people about 10 yesterday morning. The loss our Division sustained is awful, the Rifle Brigade – out of 130 men had only 35 return but however the papers will give you full particulars. I only made this scrawl to say I am all right, which I knew you would like. It was a pretty light affair for the first time of my being under fire. I

---

[1] The Great Russian Redan - one of the large Russian fortifications that ringed the city of Sebastopol and the centre of the defences attacked by the British forces.

[2] Major General John D. Johnstone – 33rd Regiment (later Colonel & Companion of the Order of the Bath).

[3] Lt. Col. George Valentine Mundy – 33rd Regiment - Field Officer.

[4] Capt. John E. Collings – 33rd Regiment – born in Guernsey 1821 and retired with rank of Major.

[5] Lt. Valentine Bennett – 33rd Regiment - age 27.

[6] Lt. Langford R. Heyland – 33rd Regiment - age 17.

[7] Brevet Major John E. T. Quayle - 33rd Regiment (Cross of the Legion of Honour) – died 1859.

[8] Capt. Thomas Wickham - 33rd Regiment – retired with rank of Major in 1862.

don't think we shall ever take the place by assault & that is the general opinion here. You will see a frightful list of officers killed or wounded which I have not time to tell you. Pretyman[1] is all right & well. Billy Tupper[2] I saw yesterday, he is a very good looking fellow and I like him, what I saw. I have to get two ponies & everything here is dear – beer is 2/- a bottle.

I send this by Mundy through Lord Raglan's[3] bag & he has [*indecipherable*]

I must stop with best love to all -
Believe me ever dearest mother your most affectionate son

Basil

[*Most pages of the above letter have been over written*]

---

[1] Brevet Major William Pretyman – 33rd Regiment.
[2] Lt. Daniel 'William' Tupper – 30th Regiment - Son of Anna Maria Tupper (nee Le Marchant) & 1st cousin to TBF.
[3] Field Marshall Lord Raglan – Commander of the British troops in Crimea.

Written by Thomas Basil Fanshawe - to his brother, John Gaspard
Fanshawe – copied by their mother.
Camp before Sebastopol
June 26th 1855

Dearest John

I suppose you have heard from my Mother how I was lucky enough
to escape the other day when the Redan was attacked. How any
officer got out of it was a wonder. I might have returned myself as
slightly wounded from a bruise on my shoulder but I thought you
would ask the army about it - it must have been a stone that struck
me or a spent grape shot, anyhow I thought I was very lucky to get
off so cheap, you never saw anything so miserable as this affair was.

Our loss has been 1600 men & 90 officers killed or wounded &
nothing gained which is the worst part. Old Wickham got hit in the
foot & has gone down to Kamiesh Bay today to proceed to England
in the 'Essex'. He suffers a good deal of pain & it will be a long time
before he is all right. Quayle was hit in the stomach & the doctors at
first said he could not possibly [get] but he's going on as well as
possible & now they seem to think he will eventually recover.
Johnstone lost his left arm, taken off halfway between the elbow &
wrist, going on well – Col. Yea[1] & Hobson[2] of the 7 Fusiliers are both
dead, the latter was in the 30th Regt at Manchester in '48. Lots of
fellows who I do not know have also been killed. We lost Bennett &
Heyland, killed as went in 11 or 12 officers & only 5 came out
untouched. Mundy got a slight flesh wound in the leg. We lost on
Sunday night poor Marsh[3] our adjutant, a nephew of the chief, shot

---

[1] Colonel Lacy Walter Giles Yea – 7th Royal Fusiliers - age 47.
[2] James St. Clair Hobson Lt. Adjt - 7th Foot (Royal Fusiliers) - Died 1st attack on the
Redan 18 June 1855.
[3] Lt. Adjutant Hans Stephenson St. Vincent Marsh – 33rd Regiment - died 24 June
1855 age 21 (serving as Assistant Engineer).

in the head & leg – he was all through from the joining of this war & noted for his coolness & pluck – he was adjutant of the trenches on Sunday night & very probably came across an exposed piece of ground when quite light. I was down with a working party engaged threading up a fresh battery the same night, but not near him.

The Russians threw some shots at us & killed one of our men, nothing was left of him but his chest & arms & a bit of his foot. It is anything but pleasant to see one of those large shells coming up, looking as if it was going to drop right on to you. It was a very grand sight to see the shot & shell going the night of the attack on the Redan – the Russians hardly returned our guns but when we got into the open, which we were obliged to do before getting to the Redan - did we not get the grape on us.

It was a hard night after it was over to see the poor fellows lying about on the ground, cut about in every way. We are all anxious to see what account Lord Raglan sent home about it & how he gets out of the scrape.

Genl Estcourt[1] died of cholera yesterday or the day before. Sir G Brown[2] is very seedy on board one of the ships of the fleet. Ditto Genl. Codrington[3], Genl. Pennefather[4] & staff have taken their departure for England - the Genl. ill. There is a story going about that a young fellow of the name of Malan[5] (7th) who was hit in five places being carried home on a stretcher was meet by Lord Raglan in the 21 gun battery who asked him where he was hit & if badly - then asked if he could tell him anything about the attack – Malan

---

[1] Major-General James B. Bucknall Estcourt – Adjutant-General.

[2] General Sir George Brown GCB, KH, PC – Commander of Light Division.

[3] General Sir William Codrington, Commander of the Light Division & British Commander-in-Chief.

[4] General Sir John Lysaght Pennefather GCB – Commander of 2nd Division.

[5] Lt. Charles H. Malan - 7th Foot (Royal Fusiliers) - sustained a severe wound on 18 June 1855.

not knowing my Lord, said "that he knew one thing that it was the first time he was ever under a heavy fire & if things were mismanaged in the way they had been that morning, he hoped it would be the last" Lord Raglan told the man carrying him to take him on.

Erskine[1] has gone home sick, all last week there was only Corbett[2] & myself as Capts to do the duty. Mansfield[3], Vacher[4] & Pretyman on the staff, Ellis[5] on the sick list, who came off yesterday. Quayle wounded, Collings now Commanding Officer - Erskine also gone home sick.

This place is interminably hot & lots of flies in the tent. Yesterday we had a dust storm which nearly both blinded & suffocated me. I rode in the [xx] with Mundy who was off-handish times, considering that there are (*in pencil* 'ought to be') 9 captains for duty on the sick list to Lord Raglan's – He is very well off for [xxxxx].

On Saturday, I rode down to Tchorguna & had a bathe in the Tchernaya – it is a very pretty ride about five miles from our camp & the country in that direction very fine. The French & Sardinians are there, it is absolutely necessary to have a horse here which I have not got at present. They are going very high, nothing decent under 25 to £30 and one must have a baggage animal as well. Col. Yea's charger fetched £110 at his sale & you have no idea what prices saddles & harness can fetch. I saw a most indifferent saddle sell at £7.10. I have my saddle & bridle. Living here is very dear – a leg of

---

[1] Capt. George P. Erskine - 33rd Regiment.

[2] Capt. Frank Corbett – 33rd Regiment.

[3] Capt. Charles E Mansfield – 33rd Regiment (later Colonel Sir - KSMG, a diplomat serving in E. Europe & S. America).

[4] Capt. Frederic Smith Vacher – 33rd Regiment (Major 1856) – attended Shrewsbury School with TBF & Dick Fanshawe.

[5] Lt. Arthur E. A. Ellis – 33rd Regiment (later Major Gen GCVO, CSI & equerry to King Edward VII).

mutton, when you can get it 12/- to 16/-, a lamb 18/-, small fowls 7/- to 10/-, geese £1. Beer two shillings a bottle and not always to be had, bread 1/- a loaf, in fact nothing is cheap here. Corbett told me its cost him £30 a month during the winter to live.
Did I tell you the sailors were very riled at not having lost more men than the artillery the other day & said let us have a few more men & we shall beat them - curious idea!!

I have not heard from any of you for the last three weeks, I hope next mail I shall. If you can send me a late Times[1] do, in fact whenever you can…

[The last page of this letter continues below although in the bound original letters it appears after the last of Dick Fanshawe's letters – presumably it was missed or found after binding]

& have one. We have a mail twice a week & send two – so you are nearly certain of hearing from me once a week, but you must not fancy if I am not able to write that anything is wrong as I may be on duty & not able to write.

Corbett I do not think will stop long, in fact all the fellows here would like to leave if they could & I do not wonder at it. The trenches are beastly work, particularly now it is so hot in the day time. I have not been on yet, the working party usually instead. I believe I must stop or shall lose the mail. Send this to the Vicarage as I cannot find time for more – with best love to all there & at Parsloes & the same to Bab & Chick who I hope are flourishing.

I am ever dear John your affectionate B

Basil

---

[1] First published 1785 as *The Daily Universal Register* - became *The Times* from 1 January 1788.

Love to Dick, tell him to write when he can, mind if you see the <u>chief</u> <u>not to tell him Marsh</u> lost his life through foolish experience. I could go on a long while about the Bosphorus & Constantinople, which last is the most filthy, stinking city in existence, had I time.

Written by Thomas Basil Fanshawe - to his sister, Helen Denison.
Camp before Sebastopol
Saturday July 7th 1855

My Dearest Helen

Many thanks for your last which I got it at the beginning of this week. I have hardly anything to tell you since my last to John. Everything is going on much the same as usual, we have had no sorties or anything out of the common, only those horrid trenches. I was down on the night of the 3rd & the next day in the rifle pit of which you have heard so much, a nice safe place as the trenches go now. We are making a new battery about 50 yards to the right of the rifle pit & the Russians shelled that pretty sharp but none of our men were hit. It is very lousy thing, work being in the same place under a blazing sun. Of course the telegraph[1] gives you all the intelligence worth having. There is a shave about that we open fire again on Monday, which I do not believe.

The more one looks at Sebastopol the less one likes it & it appears to be a succession of forts which the Russians are strengthening every day. A great number of men out here are very sick of the whole concern and would go if the authorities would let them & no one looks forward to spending another winter here (which we hear is to be the case), with any degree of satisfaction.

---

[1] The electric field telegraph was used for the first time in wartime conditions in the Crimea. Royal Engineers lay an underground cable of 7km, between Balaklava and Lord Raglan's headquarters at Khutor in February 1855. The electric telegraph revolutionized communications and when a 547km submarine cable between Balaklava and Varna was laid in April 1855, officials in London and Paris were able to communicate with their commanders in the Crimea within 24 hours. Politicians were then able to issue instruction to the Generals, about which they complained - General Sir James Simpson said 'The confounded telegraph has ruined everything'.

We had a horrendous heavy rain on Monday which cooled the air, today in fact since then it is intensely hot. I was a little seedy last week but am all right again now. We have now only 3 Captains including myself covering duty and 4 subs. Rather hard lines, one has not much to do except trenches but they are a beast in themselves.

I bought a pony six£ the other day, to carry baggage & shuffle about on him in the evening. Yesterday, I rode to Inkerman & saw the French & Russian outfit below. The day before I rode to Balaclava and got a decent dinner on board the 'Gibraltar' which brought us out.

I hope the Governor's leg is getting all right. I was glad to find that he was in such good spirits and also the Messes[1] was flourishing. I hope all your fears about the chicks has long since vanished & you are all well at Parsloes. I did not hear from any one last mail, but got a county paper[2]. I have not time to write to the Vicarage[3] this mail so you must tell them I am flourishing.

Billy Tupper I see every now & then & like him very much. He declared he will not remain another winter out here & I think he is right. In fact any one out here would not stay one hour once peace was acknowledged, of which there is no appearance. Fanshawe Gostling[4] will be lucky if he gets an appointment in the Turkish (*in pencil* army) contingent but I much doubt the authorities permitting him to take it. I thought you would all like him.

---

[1] Mother of TBF – Katherine Fanshawe (nee Le Marchant).
[2] Chelmsford Chronicle or Essex Standard.
[3] Parish Church of St. Peter & St Paul, Dagenham Essex.
[4] Son of Mary & Colonel Gostling stationed in Malta – 1st cousin to TBF.

Gaspard Tupper[1] is still away at Constantinople, he was expected here on the 30th of last month. I supposed we shall have some fresh arrivals from our depot soon but I do not want to see any friends out here. I am afraid there is no chance of our taking the field this year & so getting out of the trenches.

You must make allowances for this stupid epistle but I thought although I had nothing to tell you of[f] you would be pleased to learn I am still all right. All our wounded officers have gone away to England & more going on as well as possible. Give my love to the Governor, Messes, Edward & children & believe me to be ever,

Your most affectionate brother

Basil

It is a great thing here to get letters – if you can spare the time to write them.

---

[1] Brother of Billy Tupper and son of Anna Maria Tupper (nee Le Marchant) - 1st cousin to TBF.

Written by Thomas Basil Fanshawe - to his mother.
Camp before Sebastopol
Saturday July 13th 1855

My dearest Mother,

Yesterday I got your letter of 26th of last month and one from John of the 28th. Many thanks for yours & am glad to find that the Governor is so well, and as you do not mention yourself I conclude that you are quite right. I presume that long ere this you received my letter of about 19th June telling you that I am out of the Redan[1] business all right. Certainly I had great good luck in escaping so well. My arm, as I told you was only bruised a bit, which got all right in two of three days. I might just as well returned myself wounded as Rogers[2] & Mundy of ours, but I am glad I did not for your sakes. I have been down to the Trenches three times since & have not been touched although I must have had some near things together with the rest of the men who were down particularly during the night as then you cannot see the bits of the shell when they land. I was down last Monday at Balaclava being told that I should not be wanted that afternoon, fancy my disgust, just as I was leaving the town, meeting one of our doctors who told me I was for trenches.

I got down to the trenches about 10 o/c and had about two hours of them, but it was rather a sell, on getting down I found all my men engaged at working on a new battery in one of the [xxxxcursed] trenches & congratulated myself I should get home for one or two o/c a.m. but found myself sold as our mortars were to open fire on the Redan about 4 o/c which they did in great style & I hear knocked it about. The Russians replied gun for gun nearly & dismounted 4 of ours. I got quite out of the line of fire with the men and could not see what injury the Redan suffered from where I was. I did not get

---

[1] The first attack on the Redan 18 June 1855.
[2] Lt. John Thornton Rogers (later Lt Col Rogers DSO) – 33rd Regiment.

home to camp until 9¼ pm Tuesday night very sleepy & tired as you may imagine, not having been able to go to sleep except for a couple of hours by fits and starts in the trenches. Our guns fired away from 4 'til 10 o/c & again all afternoon & there has been a good deal of firing every night since on both sides.

I had no idea what a way bits of shell when they burst fly about. Two or three burst some 4 or 500 yards behind me in & over the 21 gun battery & bits came back quite that distance to where I was. One bit came down close, about six inches from two men, 20 yards from where I was sitting.

You ask me what I think of active service? If trenches come under that denomination, where you have to remain close under the parapet with round shot & shell coming over & round you, and not certain of your life for a moment together, unable to do anything in way of retaliation - I tell you plainly I utterly detest it. In the morning of the 18th June I did not care a bit, but the trenches are the devil. We now take the trenches by division instead of Regiment & Division. The Light Division finished the trenches last night but I got off as our Regt only has 1 Captain & I was last on the list for duty. I suppose I shall not be on again till Monday or Thursday next which is a great thing to look forward to.

There has been nothing doing since I wrote, except working at a new battery & firing at night and morning. I hear there is a report that the Army is to make an assault on the 16th which I doubt. I do not think that they will cram our Division in front again. All our wounded have left us for England & going on favourably. I am sorry to hear such bad account of the Colonel, no one here thinks he will ever rejoin. Gough[1] arrived in harbour about two days back, but

---

[1] Lt. Col. Thomas Bunbury Gough - 33rd Regiment – severely wounded at the Battle of Alma and again whilst leading his company at the Attack of the Redan - died 18 September 1855 (aged 48).

has not yet come to the front. It is much against his will I fancy that he came. Prescott[1] & Montmorency[2] arrived yesterday, which is a good thing for the subalterns, for the last ten days we have only had 6 officers doing duty, 3 Captains & 3 Subs. I wish they would send some other Captains up. Mundy's[3] wound was very trifling. I suppose <u>you</u> know who the new Commander in Chief out here is to be, we have only heard today that there is one coming out. Corbett is the only officer of the 33rd Regt who has never left the Regt since it left Dublin in '54 & about 27 men of over 1000 who left at the same time.

I got such a kind letter from Aunt Mary last mail, hoping if I was wounded, I would go straight to Malta. I should find my room ready, nothing could be kinder. She says Malta is quite deserted. Eleanor[4] has gone away for the summer, in some swell's yacht and they do not expect [her] back for some time, this I suppose you know. They seem much pleased at Fanshawe having made Dagenham his abode & obliged for your kindness to him though nothing could be kinder than they were to me. I am afraid I shall not have time to write to them this mail. I was sure you would like Fan, give him my love if he is still with you. I have written to John by this mail so you need not send him this. I wrote a line to Helen last week, a very stupid production, but it told you I was all right. Edward has I hope shook his cold off.

The camp looks to me more like a large fair than anything else and if it was not for the reports of the gun, one could hardly fancy one was in an enemy's country. Just before I arrived, the Russians took to

---

[1] Lt. Edward B. Prescott – 33rd Regiment.

[2] Lt. Raymond H. de Montmorency, 3rd Viscount Frankfort de Montmorency (later Major General) – 33rd Regiment.

[3] Confirmed by regimental records as 'slight wound'.

[4] Daughter of Mary Gostling – 1st cousin to TBF.

throwing shot & shell into our camp, but that amusement since the Mamelon[1] has been ours has stopped.

I am sorry that my using thick paper increased the postage but I was not aware of the fact. Pay your letters otherwise I shall not receive any, by the way I got hold of the papers you mentioned having despatches. This last mail, John sent me one.

I hope you have settled that ruffian Roberts one way or the other by this time and will have no more trouble with him. How does the new man suit you – well I hope.

What a sell it will be for Tom Le Marchant[2] if he finds Sir Gaspard[3] starting for Gibraltar. I hope he may get it, much better, I pray than Halifax in a pecuniary point of view.

I found the anti-cholera[4] pills you sent in the box most useful. The weather has been thundering hot & dust to any amount really stifling one, you could write your name with your finger inside my tent yesterday on anything that was there. Today we have had a heavy thunder shower which has cooled the air & laid the dust, much to my comfort. The flies bother one considerable.

---

[1] Mamelon - French name for the breast shaped hillock near Sebastopol, also adopted by the British and sometimes referred to as Gordon's Hill.

[2] Lt. Col. Thomas Le Marchant – youngest brother of TBF's mother – served in the 7th Regiment of Dragoon Guards, and later as Colonel employed as Assistant Military Secretary at Nova Scotia – Uncle to TBF.

[3] Lt-Gen Sir John Gaspard Le Marchant GCMG KCB (1803–1874) 3rd brother of TBF's mother - British Army officer and governor of Newfoundland from 1847 to 1852 – Uncle to TBF.

[4] Anti-Cholera and anti-diarrhoea pills and medicines were frequently advertised in National & local newspapers of the period - usually manufactured and sold by individual pharmacists.

I must bring this to a close & I have been interrupted so often since I began that you will be clever to make something of this.
Best love to the Governor & all at home & believe ever dearest mother,

Your most affectionate son

Basil

Written by Thomas Basil Fanshawe - to his brother, John Gaspard Fanshawe - copied by their mother.
Camp before Sebastopol
Saturday July 13th (1855)

My dearest John

Your last of the 30th June reached me yesterday. Many thanks for your long letter, I have written regularly every mail to either you, Helen & my Mother since my arrival and hope the letters have been duly received.

Everything here is going on much as usual. I mean we have had no more attacks on either side and no one seems to have an idea of what move to take. We are building a new battery for 6 or 8 guards well on our front trenches, which they seem to think will do good service and rattle at the ships in harbour.

I have been down in the trenches twice since I wrote last. I was in them on Monday night last and did not get back till 9¼ on Tuesday night. I was in hope of being able to get off to camp on the morning of Tuesday, my men having been working at the battery from 10 to two during the night, but it was no go. I had two men hit that night, one in the head from a bit of shell, a nasty wound. The other man lost two of his toes. One of the batteries opened fire on the Tuesday morning on the Redan and I believe did a deal of damage but the Russians were not slow in returning our fire & I hear dismounted 4 of our guns - some of our men (not 23) in the advanced trenches were hit by our own shells bursting. Some say it is the fault of the Artillery & the Artillery say it arises from the hardness of the shells which they borrowed from the French.

It is beastly work in the trenches at any time but particularly during the day as like it is so hot & no one can go to sleep if the guns are firing much. I with the men during the day were in a very good safe place, no one were touched although there must necessarily have been some very near escapes. One bit of shell fell close, not a foot from two men. The mortar fired from 4 in the morning till 10 and again in afternoon from 3 all the rest of that day & ever since then there has been heavy firing during the night.

We have only 6 officers fit for duty, Collings, Corbett & myself, Ellis away sick, Gracey, Donovan[1], Cox & Rogers' sub, Montmorency came up yesterday with a draft of 50 men from Malta but that is very little use to us. In fact it makes more men for duty with the same number of officers. Old Gough arrived in the 'Golden Fleece' two days ago but he has not yet made his appearance in Camp. Mundy's wound was nothing - a ball shot grazing his thigh and drawing blood, I might just as well have returned myself as wounded, but he always makes a mountain out of a mole hill! Rogers wound was just a scratch, just as if you scraped the skin getting over a fence or rather a stone wall.

I certainly was very lucky in getting out of that mess untouched and have been since, as one never knows when heading for the trenches, if you will return alive and in The Times which you sent me (many thanks for it), says it is a regular hard life. Quayle, wonderful to say has been pronounced out of danger and has gone in 'The Great Tasmania', ditto Wickham and Johnstone, the latter taking his son[2] with him, a great shame merely for the purpose of looking after his father – the boy was out here about 5 weeks & of course with our reduced numbers throws harder work on the Subs. Out of 1100 men & 33 officers of the 33rd Regt who left Dublin March '54, Corbett is the only officer who has never been away from his duty, and about 27 men are all that remain of the old hands. It is rather staggering to think over. Wickham's wound will, the doctors say, take at least (6)

---

[1] Lieutenant Henry George Donovan – 33rd Regiment.
[2] Ensign John Douglas Johnstone – aged 19.

months to get well and everyone thinks he is very lucky to get out of this place.

I need not say everyone is horridly bored with this life & a good many would leave if they could. I am not now talking of our people, but the whole army, especially as we have the prospect of another winter before us. Collings has not the slightest intention of going - Lord Raglan's funeral[1] cortege to Kamiesh Bay was, I hear a very fine sight. Being for the trenches that day I missed seeing it.

Sebastopol is a nice clean looking place, built of white stone and seems with the exception of the barracks to show little sign of being hammered at for the last 8 or 10 months. Poor Hobson was certainly a most unlucky fellow he was shot close to Wickham, his thigh smashed and he could not stand the operation after it was over. He was at Malta while I was there. I do not believe he was happy as I know the lady, the wife of a man of the 49th was the reason. He refused the ship which was to take him <u>to the Crimea</u> not to England, (was) on account of the badness of the accommodation on board. Old Gough refused to go up for the same reason.

I am sorry to hear such bad accounts of the Colonel (Blake)[2] I hope he will get over it all right but I doubt his ever regressing. Tom Pakenham[3] is a deal better at home laid up than out here. Pretyman had an attack of cholera (slight) on Monday morning but was right in two days. I was very seedy for a couple of days with diarrhoea but am now all right, this was 10 days back.

---

[1] Death from dysentery and clinical depression on 29 June 1855 - his body brought to England for burial.

[2] Brevet-Colonel 'Fred' Blake CB – 33rd Regiment - died of 'fever' 23rd August 1855 shortly after returning home.

[3] Thomas Henry Pakenham, son of Lt.-Gen. Hon. Sir Hercules Robert Pakenham & nephew of the Duke of Wellington.

I have seen nothing of Billy Tupper for a week at least, he is a nice fellow and good looking. Gaspard has not yet returned from Scutari[1], at least I have not heard of his arrival. Carr's[2] brother[3] in the 49th I see now and then, he seems to me a better sort of fellow than most.

Some of the 18 Royal Irish on the day of the attack on the Redan got into some of the houses near the cemetery, got themselves drunk on cherry brandy which they discovered and took a door down, put it outside and began to dance jigs, one of them was spotted by the Russians so they took down some damask curtains wrapped him up and left him on the sofa – another was wounded who they brought down on a Broadwood[s][4] grand piano & lots of Guinea pigs, pigeons or anything they could lay hands on. Among other things a child of about 3 or 4 years old - on being asked why they brought it said 'sure the Mother had three of them and could we take them all'. It was sent back after living on ration pork and rum for three days in their camp.

---

[1] Florence Nightingale's nursing administration centre was based in The Barrack Hospital at Scutari - a district of Constantinople located on the Asian shore of the Bosphorus opposite the peninsula of Stamboul.
[2] Lt. J. Carr - 33rd Regiment – arrived in Crimea January 1855, wounded in November that year and returned to England February 1856.
[3] Capt. Ralph Edward Carr – 39th Regiment – later promotions to Colonel of the 36th Regiment in 1881 – awarded the Légion d'Honneur.
[4] Broadwood of London founded in 1728 – oldest surviving piano makers in the world.

I am glad to hear the Govr and Messus are so fresh. I wish I was back again with you all, but I am afraid unless wounded it will be some time before that happy event will take place – I hope that scoundrel Roberts has either paid up or cleared out & Gilmore[1] may buy the living[2].

The weather has been very hot the last week and generally hottest from 4 to 8 in the morning when a breeze generally springs up. This morning we have had a short refreshing, cooling thunder storm, which has laid the dust, with which we were nearly stifled yesterday. This bothers one awfully of a morning in bed. I think I told you I have got a pony for six pounds, which does what I want, riding about in the afternoon. It is no beauty but quite good enough for baggage.

Balaclava is a favourite resort with most here or Karani 2 miles nearer to camp where most of the sultans reside. Things keep up, I paid 19/- a dozen for [xxx] today – I went on board the 'Gibraltar', the ship which brought us out to Malta, the Capt made me a present of half a cwt of potatoes, a great haul as on the average they cost £1 a piece.

I am afraid I shall try your patience if I go on (crossing) much more so with best love to Bab and Chick who I hear from every one is a

---

[1] Rev. John Gilmore, Curate of Dagenham - Electors Registration List 1855 states his main address as 8 Brunswick Square, London but residing at 'freehold cottages, near the church'. Eventually the Living was not bought by him; soon after he settled in Kent as the Rector of the Holy Trinity Church in Ramsgate. He became deeply involved in the men and work of the Ramsgate lifeboat, promoting their pioneering work and his initiative lead to the formation of the National Lifeboat Service. In 1874 he wrote and published 'Storm Warriors or the Lifeboat Work on the Goodwin Sands' (no longer in print but available online via Project Gutenberg).
[2] 'The Living' - the position of Vicar of Dagenham - TBF's father was the incumbent vicar and also the patron of the Living. This correspondence reveals how 'The Governor' had failing health and his obvious wish to retire and sell the living.

magnificent child, I am glad to find they are so well and fresh.
Believe me Dearest John I am your most affectionate brother
Basil

Love to Dick, I have not heard from him for an age – you have no
idea how one comes across fellows out here, who one has not met
for a long time - the 97 Regt & the 72 are both here & old friends of
mine.

Tell me when you write again if I shall [xxx] my letter.

Written by Thomas Basil Fanshawe - to his brother, John Gaspard
Fanshawe - copied by their mother.
Saturday July 20th (1855)

My dearest John,

On my return from the trenches last night where I had the pleasure
of passing the last 24 hours, I was very glad to find your letter & one
from my Mother. I don't think I should have written this mail, as I
have so little to tell you, if both of you had not said how glad you
would be to hear. I am all right and hope to continue so & I am glad
to say that we have had very few casualties, none among the
officers. The Russians made a sortie on Tuesday night & were driven
back with a loss of about 50. Last night as the shave goes, a party of
Russian Artillery men mistook their way into the Malakoff & got in
front of their own guns & the Russians inside either thought these
men were going to desert or took them for French, just in the dusk
obliged at them. We did the same, ditto the French, consequently as
you may imagine they rather caught it & 30 of them were left on the
ground. I forgot to say, the Russians were artillery men.

The French are to be ready so they say, in about 12 days, which I
suppose means that a bombardment will commence again. Their
advance trench is within 100 metres of the Malakoff. I hear that we
are to move a good many guns from the old 21 gun battery to the
front & make another heavy battery there. When I was down the
other night they tried throwing the carcases again, which was a
failure, the first burst in the muzzle and showered the bits on our
own men (the object of carcasses is to set the town on fire). I am
rather glad for my own sake that they did not go on with them as
our own men were just behind the battery and in all probability we
should have been shelled severely. Fancy a shell bursting between a
man's legs of the 88th or 77th and doing him no harm, beyond

burning out his coat and hair severely and burning the man's ammunition pouch half through, that was a near touch!

Montmorency, one of our fellows, yesterday morning was in the trenches, sitting down to eat his breakfast, he had his plate on his knee when a bullet which must have been a spent one, hit his plate and smashed it to atoms, without hitting him.

There has been a good deal of firing this afternoon but I don't know on whose side, but most likely both. Gaspard Tupper arrived from Scutari on Monday last & came up to me with Billy on Tuesday. I do not think he is nearly so good looking as I remember him. He says he is all right as does Billy. The Carrs are all right, I have just seen the 37th men here. We hear that their Col (Blake) has expressed his determination to sell. I am sorry to hear such bad accounts of him and think from what you say the sooner he recovers the money to his family the better.

I should be delighted to see Dick out here, camp life will rather astonish him. My Mother says she also would like to see it, I wonder how long she would remain. I am so glad to find you are all so well. I wish I could see you all again or had the prospect of so doing. We all expect to winter out here unless we get into Sebastopol before the winter sets in – I certainly hope we may get in and that I may be able to pull through the scrimmage of getting in, which will be no joke. On Sunday, if I am not for the trenches I am going with a large party to Kamiesh Bay to dine. I have not been there yet.

I wish we could get some more Capts as if we send two Capts to the trenches there are only 3 of us and it only gives us two nights & four in bed alternately. It is such a farce to see Johnstone who never left the trench on the 17th, mentioned in despatches. I think I told you Gough did arrive on Saturday last. The French had a [low] in front of the Mamelon on Sunday night and gave the Russians a (dusting).

I got no letters which you mention I ought to have received on arrival here – one letter of my Mother's had gone to Malta from here and back – its date June 8th. I hope you will send this to my Mother.

With best love to you and Bab & Chick,
Believe me dearest John your most affectionate brother

Basil

Thanks for the papers which arrived all right.

Written by Thomas Basil Fanshawe - to his mother.
Camp before Sebastopol
Saturday July 27th 1855

My dearest Mother

Last night I got your letter of July 9th with Times & County Chronicle, & letter from John of the 14th with a 'Times' of the 14[th.] - Many thanks to you both. I missed the last two mails, not that I would have had much to communicate as things are going on much as usual. We [xxxxxing] up to the Redan and the French up to Malakoff. The last two days I have been rather seedy from a bilious attack, but I hope to be all right by tomorrow. I was in the trenches last Thursday week, came in that night after 24 hours, on again on Saturday, off at 2 then Sunday morning and again on Wednesday but got off on Thursday morning early, and this I fancy has contributed more to making me seedy than anything. Corbet and myself being the only two Captains, Collings having hurt his knee and Ellis on the sick list.

I think we shall have either a good deal of promotion or stay as we are for a long time, the Col cannot remain, Mundy talks of substantive rank and I should much doubt many of our wounded staying in the service. Lacy[1] I hear is going to exchange to Ceylon. Gough and Erskine, I cannot think will stop, so if I escape the Russian shot & shell, I may have a chance of promotion. Is not Mundy a lucky boy to get C.B.? There is a shave aboard that all the officers who were out last winter are on the 1st November to get 3 months leave for England and no doubt they deserve it but I fear their number will be few if we have to attack the town again. I heard this Thursday that the French would not be ready for any grand shine for a month.

---

[1] Captain Richard Lacy – 33rd Regiment – born in Guernsey. Promoted to Inspector of Musketry in May 1856, and later in North America.

Yesterday and today there has been a good deal of firing, mostly on the French. When in the trenches on Sunday night, the Russians asked for a flag of truce to bury their dead, killed in a sortie two nights previous. This was refused by the French who playfully reminded the Russians that when they were granted a flag of truce the time before, the Russians remark was how they could have been such fools to grant it. However the Russians came out to try to collect their dead and for ten minutes there was very heavy firing, and an awful row, it was very fine to see our guns firing their gun shells right into where one supposed the Russians to be.

Our weather has been very amiable, stifling dust storms and thunderstorms, the latter much to be preferred of the two, and two nights back it rained the whole night, much to everyone's delight. Nobody seems pleased at the prospect of wintering out here, I do not wonder at it. I think in my last I told you we take the trenches by divisions which with only two captains gives us only two nights in bed.

Both the Tuppers came and paid me a visit this afternoon, both looking fresh and well. Billy thinks he will not remain here after 1st November. They told me of Robert Le Marchant[1] getting most likely a good curacy at last, I hope he will not be disappointed. Young Hewett is in the 4th Division, on the extreme left some two miles away from our camp. I think I saw him one night at the Gostlings and thought he was a rough customer, but I may have made a mistake. I heard from Aunt Mary last mail and replied to her. You ask how one spends the time, generally going down to Balaclava on a foraging expedition. I was down yesterday, thinking the ride can put me to rights, but it did not. I got on board a Turkish ship, 3 turkeys at 5/6 each, 2 geese at 3/ 4 each, which for Balaclava was not dear. Fancy my having to pay 3/- a pot for Marmalade – small, 9/-

---

[1] Robert Le Marchant, Rector of Little Rissington 1862-1915 (b.1819).

for 8 plates of the commonest description and small tumblers at a shilling each. I also paid 6/6 each for pressed tongues. I got a great haul the other day – a sheep for £1-10[s]. If you could send me a box containing a few of the following items, I should think myself supplied like a Prince: a round of spiced beef tongues, hams, tea, sugar, potted soups, jams, and if possible a cask of beer as this last commodity cost 19/- a (keg).

I think if young Bayliff[1] has not left the depot, the best plan would be to ask him to drop you a line when he is likely to leave Ireland and to have the things sent to our old friend Thompson, requesting him to have the things put on board the ship Bailiff goes in, if this could be arranged without any trouble it will be a good arrangement to supply to our establishment.

I was with our Adjutant Trent[2] who was affected on poor Marsh's death. I was sorry to hear that Robert's contract about the living was broken off, what a ruffian he must be and ditto that scoundrel Anderson, but John tells me that accounts from Lancashire[3] are flourishing.

My [xxxx] of a pony for six pounds does me well enough. Last Sunday a party of 10 of us rode to Kamiesh Bay and dined at a French café, we had really a most excellent dinner, lots of champagne, claret, soda water with coffee, cigars etc for 16/ bob a piece, not dear. The Bay seems just as crowded as Balaclava, only more order in the former.

---

[1] Richard Lane Bayliff – 33rd Regiment - Son of Rev. T. T. L. Bayliff, of Albury, born 1833 served in 33rd Regiment during the Crimean War, transferred to the 100th Regiment, promoted to Captain and retired 1870.
[2] Lt. John Trent – 33rd Regiment - sustained a severe wound in the Final Attack on the Redan - 8 September 1855.
[3] Swineshead, Wyersdale – the Fanshawe estate in the North of England.

Send this on to John, I am not fresh enough today to write another stupid epistle, both the Carrs are very flourishing and are in the same hut with me while writing this. I shall write to him by Tuesday mail next, I must drop my pen. With very best love to you all at Parsloes, John, Bab, Dick, the Govr and yourself.

Tell Dick if he does not write I shall expect to see him out here.

Goodbye, dearest Mother and believe me to be your most affectionate son,

Basil

Written by Thomas Basil Fanshawe - to his brother, John Gaspard Fanshawe - copied by their mother.
Camp before Sebastopol
July 31st (1855)

Dearest John

I have not a word to tell you as I have been on the sick list since writing last with a bilious attack, when I tell you I have not ate or smoked for a week you may imagine it was no pleasing affair, however I am today a good better and hope soon to be all right again. Many thanks for your last of the 14th July and Times of same date. I tried hard to answer it on Tuesday last but my head was in such a whirl I could not.

There is nothing fresh since my last, except a report of 16,000 Russians having arrived which I believe is the case. The Frenchman who was exchanged the other day has been living during the period of his imprisonment (if you can so call it) up the country. He says all the Russian soldiers worth anything are before Sebastopol. Those where he was, were miserable wretches and half their fire locks would not go off. The French soldier said they treated him well, gave him 20 sous a day and did not ask him to work.

I am very sorry to hear Edward and Helen leave Parsloes, evidently too long in one spot is not their maxim. I should not have inflicted you with this stupid scrawl but I thought you might all be fancying all sorts of misery if I did not write having said in my last that I was seedy.

My best love to all & believe me dearest John your very affectionate brother

Basil

Written by Thomas Basil Fanshawe - to his brother, John Gaspard Fanshawe - copied by their mother.
Camp before Sebastopol
August 6th 1855

My dearest John

I have been on the sick list the whole of the past week & on Friday when I ought to have written to catch the mail the Dr made me remain in my tent on my bed & even if he had not told me to rest quiet I should have been unable to write. I was so dreadfully seedy, in fact I do not recollect being touched up with this sort of thing before, generally waking with a head ache, my tongue feeling too large for my mouth and seedy all over. I have been living on bread and milk for the last 4 days, it is the only thing I can eat. I am taking quinine[1] 3 times a day, most horrid stuff. I am still on the sick list & expect to remain on it till the end of the week. I am as weak as possible, in fact I had no idea I should have been pulled down so much in so short a time. Our Surgeon says it's only what most people on arriving out here have to go through to get acclimatised - I am decidedly better this morning.

On Friday last I received your letter also one from my Mother and Helen, many thanks for them and also The Times of 20th. I received a whole heap of Bells Life[2] from Den and a Chronicle. How is it that I never get any letters on Mondays, that is today and they all arrive on Friday. Last Friday's mail brought me a letter from my Mother of the 18th & one from you of the 21st so I cannot help thinking there is a mistake somewhere.

---

[1] In the fight against Malaria, large scale use of quinine started around 1850 although its medicinal values had been known and used for many centuries before.
[2] Bell's Life in London & Sporting Chronicle - weekly sporting pink broadsheet paper, published 1822-1886.

I was glad to find the Chick's[1] attack passed off and that he is all right again. How I envied my Mother's account of the strawberries at the Vicarage!

We had a regular wet day on Thursday last, the ground was mud 3 inches thick. I did nothing but shiver & shake the whole day I never was more miserable or had a more determined attack of the devils. Friday arrived - we had a very hot sun, which by no means helps me on. Corbett has at last gone home on 3 months leave. He left without the slightest intention of returning to there (dressings) unless his friends at home persuade him to do so. Collings is still on the sick list & is honestly riled at several men junior to him having been made Brevet Major. John is quite as much entitled to one as Don Donovan[2]. Ellis came back from the trenches this morning sick, so we have not a single Capt to do duty. Corbett intends to look you up on arrival.

There is a report that we are to have another shy at the Redan about the middle of this month. The French and 4000 Sardinians (so they say) are to make another attempt at the Malakoff – of course we know nothing about it certain - but I shall not be surprised if they shoved our own division in the front again, if they do I hope I shall have the luck to pull through – the Russians made a sortie about Friday last & took the heavy defence from the 39th. General Carr of the 39th was in charge of the party & as he had only a few men with him he retired according to orders free of injury incurred. There was a large fire in town last night but it is a matter of doubt if we or the Russians set it on fire.

---

[1] Evelyn John Fanshawe, born 22 July 1854, eldest child of TBF's brother John and his wife Barbara Coventry.

[2] Captain Edward Westby Donovan – 33rd Regiment – severely wounded at Sebastopol.

Two of our men died of the Cholera two days back but I believe it is not spreading.

I am too seedy to write more this mail, with love to Bab and all at the Vicarage & Parsloes.

I am always your most affectionate brother

Basil

Send this on – I saw the Tuppers yesterday, all were kindly.

P.S.

I feel a good deal better tonight. The mail today brought me the express of 21 June – the latest report is that the authorities here have telegraphed for huts - reply sent back is if not successful in the next attack, take the Army from the Crimea. I don't believe a word of this.

Goodbye, dear John - I hear <u>we</u> set the town on fire…

Written by Thomas Basil Fanshawe - to his brother, John Gaspard Fanshawe - copied by their mother.
Camp before Sebastopol
August 10th 1855

Dearest John

I have been a good deal worse than what I told you in my previous letters, I mean I did not like to say how really seedy I was for fear of alarming you – but I do not recollect ever having been so touched up before and although now I am a good deal better & am getting around, still the Drs say I shall do no good here – they have given me leave to the 10th September. So tomorrow I start for Therepia[1] on the Bosphoras (nominally) but if I can I shall try going down to Malta & back, if possible. I fancy a sea trip will do more good than anything, when I tell you that I have not eaten bread or smoked for the last fortnight you can form an opinion that I have not been A1.

The afternoon I received your letter of the 28th of last month. I wrote last Friday and Tuesday to let you know how I was going on – the last letter I numbered & shall continue to do so as then it will be easy for you to find if all my valuable epistles reach. I suppose maybe Dick will have started long before this reaches, but if he has not, tell him if he arrives at Constantinople before the 10 of next month to enquire at the Post Office where I am, as if I remain in Therepia I shall stop my letters at the Office & shall leave word in case he calls, where I am to be found.

I should think I have been long enough on the subject of self. Everything here is progressing in the same old style, now our trenches are so near the Russians that our casualties are getting more numerous. We had three more hit yesterday, two badly. They

---

[1] A district of Istanbul located on the European shoreline of the Bosphorus strait, where the foreign embassies had their summer houses during the Ottoman period.

say that 200 mortars have arrived in Kamiesh Bay for the French & they are all to be placed in position before we attack again. Neither I or any other member of this camp ever heard of the expedition pulling out of Balaclava – the firing has been very heavy lately, particularly at dusk. Capt Montagu[e][1] of the Engineers who was to have taken them over March last, has been sent back - he was taken through the Redan and he describes it as almost impregnable, but I do not see why we should attack that particular spot again. The Russians say they do not care for our sentrical fire, this I do not believe. Montagu[e] also says the Russians told him they had no idea our men made such bad sentries as in the winter they used to run in and out of the ~~piquet~~ sentries to discover the strength of our piquets. This I believe may also come under the head of <u>Bosh</u>. We had a thunder storm two days ago which cooled the sun & ground, today the heat is awful and fries & bothers one to death.

The Gov wrote to me by this mail and again much obliged for his epistle which I shall answer as soon as I have settle where I go for the month & let him know my plans. I also heard from my Mother. I am glad to find they are both so flourishing & well. How I would like to see you all again. I am sorry the Denisons have given notice to quit. I thought till they had actually done so there was a chance of them remaining. I should hope there will be no difficulty in finding a tenant after so much money laid out on the place. I hope you will have a jolly time in the country & have some good shooting.

Evelyn I hear from every one is a very fine child & admired by all who see him. No doubt the country will do him much good.

---

[1] Horace W. Montagu (1823 - 1916) Captain in Royal Engineers was reported missing in action during minor actions at Sebastopol - 22 March 1855. Recipient of the Legion of Honour and the order of Merit of Sardinia, he retired in 1887 as Colonel Commandant of the Royal Engineers having been knighted and awarded K.C.B.

We have heard nothing of Simpson[1] leaving, recalled or about his giving up the Commander-in-Chiefship – Gen Eyre[2] is I hear detested by his officers, as to his losing his leg that is all nonsense, I believe he has the use of his limbs as much as I have of mine.

Today I received the second edition of the Times of the 27th - many thanks, today your letter which is dated a day later – my Mother sent me by this mail an Illustrated[3] and a county paper. I think I have answered all your letters from the end of June very regularly & I have generally written once a week in reply to one of the family. I will write again soon.

I think Col. Blake will exchange & so the step will go out of the Regt, such is the opinion here. We had a large draft arrive today, Subaltern of the name of Ball - & 12 men!

Goodbye with love to all, your affectionate brother

Basil

Send this to the Vicarage - I hope my mother will not faint at my modest request for eatables made in my last.

I have not seen the Tuppers since Monday.

---

[1] General Sir James Simpson GCB (1792 – 1868). Sent to the Crimea in February 1855 to act as chief of staff to Lord Raglan. Subsequently he took command after the death of Raglan on 28 June 1855 until he resigned in November 1855, when he was succeeded by Sir William Codrington.
[2] Major General Sir William Eyre KCB, former aide de camp to Queen Victoria, in 1854 commanded the 3rd Brigade and later the 3rd Division in Crimea. Appointed commander of Her Majesty's forces in British North America during 1855 but with broken health following action in Crimea, he resigned in June 1859 and he died within three months.
[3] Illustrated London News – published from 1842 (the world's first illustrated newspaper).

'Hospital in Sebastopol - Dr Durgan attending the wounded', *an engraving from a sketch by E. A. Goodall*

Illustrated London News 6th October 1855

Florence Nightingale (1820 - 1910)
Social reformer, statistician
and founder of
modern nursing.

Wikimedia Commons

Mary Seacole (1805 - 1881)
Nurse and hotelier in Crimea who gave
assistance to wounded soldiers
on the battlefield.

Wikimedia Commons

Vivandière
Women attached to French military regiments
as general assistants

Roger Fenton, 1855
Library of Congress

Written by Thomas Basil Fanshawe – to his father, Thomas Lewis Fanshawe – copied by his mother.
On board Screw Ship[1] Charity
No 140
August 24th (1855)

My Dearest Governor,

Many thanks for your last letter which I received the day before I left camp. On the 19th of the month I wrote to John & told him I was going away on a month's leave as I was very seedy & pulled down from an attack of [bilious] fever & as I got no better up in front the Dr. told me I had better go away for a little & as I thought they ought to know best I followed their advice & came down to Scutari with the intention of going on the Bosphorus to Therepia.

I left Balaklava on the 12th in the 'Poitiers' a sailing ship towed down by the 'Ottawa'[2] & reached Constantinople on the Tuesday about the middle of the day, but we did not land till the Thursday & very glad I was to leave the ship as I was nearly eaten up with the fleas, bugs & all sorts of pleasant animals of that species. There was not the

---

[1] Early steamships were driven by paddle, which became the de facto means of propulsion. However, experiments with a screw propeller date from Ancient Greece and Archimedes. Interest in the Archimedes screw was renewed by British inventors John Ericsson and Francis Pettit Smith who found that the screw doubled the speed attainable from a small steam engine which proved viable for modern use. The first screw ship, SS *Archimedes*, was launched in 1838 utilising the screw design of Smith's original patent and the ship had a profound influence on Isambard Kingdom Brunel - leading to the SS *Great Britain*, the first steam screw ship to cross the Atlantic in 1845.
[2] Built by John Baird & Co of Birkenhead in 1854 the *Ottawa*, owned by the Canadian Steam Navigation Co was iron hulled, 1,275 ton and accommodated 100 passengers. In the same year she made only four crossings from Liverpool to Quebec & Montreal before being requisition for troop transport to the war in Crimea. In 1855, the *Ottawa* was sold to the P & O Line for routes to the Middle East and India.

slightest accommodation for washing in the cabins, in fact I was never on board a worse (French) ship. I of course thought beds would be provided but they were not, so I had to sleep on a straw mattress with a couple of blankets, not the coolest or most agreeable covering when the blankets are new – on arrival I found the medical officer at Scutari who came on board made some difficulty about my going up to Therepia as in general orders. I was down for Scutari so I went to the Palace Hospital[1] there, from that I was also very glad to get away as I found myself getting no stronger - in fact going back, which I attributed to the low unhealthy situation of the hospital & the most horrid smell from the drains all day & all night. I applied to go to Therepia & got leave on Tuesday morning.

Just as I was starting & was having my portmanteau put in one of the Turkish carriages (considered contrivances for jolting you to death) the doctors came in & said that a steamer was going down to Malta that afternoon & any sick officers who thought they would be benefitted by the voyage there & back, he would recommend for a passage. Only three officers accepted the offer, I being one of the three, leave was granted & we came on board this ship, a most comfortable one, that afternoon and left that night & stopped the next day in the Dardenelles at a place called Chanak Kalehsi[2], in English, City of Plates – to land some 200 pack saddles for the Land Transport Corps. This delayed us till 12o/c on Wednesday, when we left & have made a good time as far as this. We passed Cape Matapan last night & expect to reach Malta tomorrow night. I shall then surprise the Gostlings, if they are there. I feel a good deal better and sharper than I did at the Palace Hospital & by the time I get back I expect to be all right again.

---

[1] One of the smaller military hospitals at Scutari administered by Florence Nightingale from late 1854.

[2] Now called Çanakkale, this old Ottoman Turkish city is the nearest major town to the site of ancient Troy. Situated on two continents, it lies on the Asian coast of the Dardanelles, at the narrowest point.

I stopped my letters at the Post Office but came away in such a hurry I had not time to call & see if there were any – I suppose I shall find numbers on my return – my stay at Malta will not be long as my leave is up on 10th September.

I hope you will have good sport in the 1st, I wish I could join you. I can give no news from the front except what you already know about the French and Sardinians hitting the Russians on the Tchernaya – 900 prisoners came past Constantinople on Monday and I should not wonder if we had by this time made another assault on the town. I hope this attack will prove more successful than the last, I shall much regret being absent should it have come off.

Generally & today the heat is intense & Malta I expect will be like an oven. I shall lay in a good supply of provisions for the Crimea there, & also invest capital in a goat for milk, you have no idea what luxury milk is considered in fact - I ought to get a capital goat for 15/ bob.

I was very sorry to hear of Den's departure from Parsloes but with the improvements since they arrived & a station near Barking, the difficulty of obtaining clerical will not be lessened. I suppose the old place is looking in all its glory, the garden blooming with flowers – you have no conception how I revelled in grapes and figs at Scutari. The grapes I slated in the Sultan's garden[1] at the back of the Palace, much to the disquiet of a Turk who was there on guard over the garden & who could not speak English – he came up nearly frantic at seeing myself & another officer with a large bunch of grapes in our hands.

I went to the Bazaar at Steboul once & got regularly shut up, doubled up I may say, on my way back to the boats to cross over. I suppose I went out too soon in the sun, thinking I was sharper than I was in reality. What ruffians these Turkish fellows in the Bazaar are, one fellow asked £3 for a pair of slippers and ended up getting 5 pair for £4. Another asked me 3/- for a turban for a hat & seemed perfectly happy when I gave him 1/6d. The proper way, I believe is to give about a third of what they ask.

I shall leave this open in case of anything happening before I reach Malta. How jolly it would be to meet Dick there.

---

[1] A vivid 'pictorial image' of the Sultan's garden & Constantinople has been left by Hans Christian Anderson - *'The whole Sea of Marmora lay before us, lighted up by the rays of the moon, and in the mid-distance Scutari stood forth, its minarets gleaming with many lamps like those of Constantinople. The Mosque of St. Sophia with its four, and the Mosque of Ahmed with its six minarets, stood forth in especial splendour, each pinnacle crowned with a double or a triple garland of glittering stars. They seemed to surround the garden of the Serail, which stretched down towards the Bosphorus, dark as a starless night. No light shone in the palace of the sultanas near the shore; but there where the Golden Horn ends, a sword of flame had been reared, that threw a ruddy glow over the waters'.* (Stories for the Household -1889).

We lost a number of transports going up to Balaclava on Tuesday August 28th!

I arrived at the Gostlings yesterday and have taken up my abode here. They are all kindness, I am greatly improved (with each day) & shall be here till next week.

With love to the Messes and all at Parsloes

Believe me, I am your affectionate son

Basil

Written by Thomas Basil Fanshawe - to his brother, John Gaspard
Fanshawe.
On board 'Columbo' 61
At Constantinople
September 16 1855

My Dearest John,

I left Malta on Tuesday last, my leave expired on Monday last the
10th – the day after Sebastopol was taken. There are numerous
shaves here about the transaction but nothing official has yet come
down. I [here] the Crimea is again a sea of mud owing to the wind &
rain. I am very sorry that I was not present at the taking of the place
but perhaps if I had been I might instead of writing this scrawl laid
three feet of clay over me - more likely, all for the best.

I wrote to the Governor from Malta & have not written since not
having anything to tell you. I am flourishing and I hope now to
remain so. I lived with the Gostlings all the time & nothing could be
kinder & I enjoyed myself very much, the heat was awful. I rather
expected to see Dick before I left however he will come in plenty of
time to see Sebastopol or rather the remains of it & our trenches.

You no doubt will have received by this an official account of us all,
our information is mostly shaves, I will not bore you with it. I went
to the Post Office today (Sunday) & found it shut but if we do not
proceed till tomorrow afternoon I shall make an effort to get all my
letters which as I wished them to be sent from camp, I hope to find a
good lot.

From what I hear, I am much afraid the Light Division were in the
thick of it again. Ellis & Prescott of ours, who I saw were wounded
before leaving Malta, were I hope out of it. This has been awful grim
& if what we hear is true, 164 officers have fallen.

I got one letter from my Mother the Sunday after arriving at Malta & that is the only epistle I have got since I left camp on 10th August. This ship 'Columbo'[1] is a very fine one and is taking out shot shell (which thank God will not be wanted any longer for the trenches), huts & officers of the Turkish contingent - <u>a queer lot very</u>.

I had a very fine picnic at Malta given by the East Kent Militia.

Best love to Bab and Chick, it seems an age since I have seen your post. Fancy Erskine married to Mary Slater[2] at Carlisle, you recollect her – & poor Blake dead! How did he leave his family, well off?

Love to all at home, I will write again as soon as I arrive in Camp. Perce is rather more filthy than when last here.

Ever your most affectionate brother

Basil

---

[1] P&0 steam-engined ship launched in 1854 to carry passengers to Alexandra, Requisitioned for troop transporting to Crimea, she made three voyages from Southampton but spent most of the war period on the Black Sea towing sailing ships along the Crimean coast.

[2] George Erskine married Frances Ellen Slater in Carlisle (3 Quarter) 1855 (TBF may have confused her first name with that of Mary Moir, married to a brother officer Henry Knight Erskine).

Written by Thomas Basil Fanshawe - to his mother.
Camp before Sebastopol
September 24th (1855)

My Dearest Mother

I arrived here on Friday last and found about 40 letters from you, John, Helen & Edward, not having received one during my absence except one of yours at Malta. I am all right again. In the first place let me thank you very much for your kind present of eatables which Dick is bringing me up, will you also thank John for tobacco and Edward & Helen for the beer. I should writing myself but having been to parade this morning and since then written myself & three court martial - my time is limited. I shall write next mail.

I hope the Gov got my letter from Malta. Nothing could be kinder than the Gostlings were and I was very sorry to leave them. I should have had no difficulty in getting another month's leave but I thought it was hardly fair upon the captains up here, but I do not think that they would have showed the same consideration to me. I am sorry to have escaped the fall of Sebastopol, but console myself with the idea that had I been present I might have been shot. Poor old Gough[1] died of his wounds & was buried the day before I arrived. Young Donovan was also shot and hardly any of our people escaped without a wound of some sort, but they are all going on right. Ellis and myself are still the only captains here, Collings having gone down sick to Scutari, Mundy is also away sick, having missed Sebastopol but is expected back tonight.

I went into Sebastopol on Saturday & the pounding the town had gone through was something curious to look at. Of course, the Redan was an object of great interest to me having had one shy at

---

[1] 'Danger Wound' received in Final Attack on the Redan, 8 September 1855 - died 10 days later.

the infernal place & everyone agrees in saying that it was perfect murder sending men at the Redan the last time, as the Malakoff completely commanded it & would have swept it clean of men. The Russians had underground barracks bomb-proof so that only gunners were exposed to our fire and all say that our having got possession of the place is a great piece of luck & the Russians cannot yet realise having lost the place - if we may judge of their deserters account.

Peter is all right but had a narrow shave, the last journey a shot having gone through the back of his coat. The 2nd & Light Division are to remain here at present, in all probability for the winter. The great mistake made was sending in those two divisions who were repulsed before at it (the Redan) again. I hear everyone anticipates a [xxxjunary] shine on the Tchenaya before very long & there are numerous reports of the Russians clearing out from the North side which I doubt, as I was lying off with the fleet in the 'Colombo' for a day before incoming to Balaclava & saw them as busy as bees with their earthworks on that side.

Bunbury[1] of the 22nd who was my Captain at Perth is here & seemed very glad to see me. I must stop till tomorrow as I am going to dine with Billy Tupper & have no time to lose. I saw him & Gaspard in Sebastopol on Saturday. Billy's division I know was not engaged in the 8th affair but of course he comes in for whatever the country gives for the taking.

I have just returned from Billy's dinner & met some of the 50th men who were at (Torquay) with me. Dick I hear is at Constantinople

---

[1] Henry William Bunbury – 33rd Regiment - (born Sept.1812) promoted to Captain in 33rd Regiment July 1839. Regimental Archives list as promoted to unattached Majority in 1852 and also confirm service from 1839 in New South Wales and other areas of Australia.

and I expect him up every day. I got by today's mail your letter of the 10th Sept - many thanks for it.

Tuesday 25th morning - I have just been woke by the Sergt for letters & am afraid if I do not close this I shall miss the mail. I wrote to John from Constantinople on the 16th which I hope he got. Will you tell him in answer to his enquiries about John Hall[1], son of one of the Lancashire tenants that he died on board the steam ship 'Andes'[2] on the way from Varna here September 6th 1854, from cholera. I should have answered this long ago had I received his letter containing the query.

Billy Tupper told me you had gone over to Guernsey. I hope you both enjoyed yourselves. Milly[3] I have not seen since Malta. Yesterday we had an importation of 7 young officers but no Captain. I came up with Tom Pakenham 30th from Constantinople, a mutual friend of John & myself. He told me that the docks bill had passed and that the Gov ought to get £25000 or £30000[4] – I hope so.

---

[1] Most probably: Private J Hall - 23rd Foot (Royal Welsh Fusiliers) - who is officially listed as 'Killed in Action' at the Battle of Alma - 20 September 1854. - TBF implies that death occurred from Cholera on board the troop ship before arrival at Crimea. It is known that a disastrous situation unfolded when it became apparent that Varna, despite being on the Black Sea coast, was a very unhealthy place and many man died of cholera and diarrhoea before they reached the battlefields. Possibly information was officially 'blurred' causing this tenant farmer on the estate in Lancashire to appeal to the Fanshawe family to help get clarification on the cause of his son's death.

[2] *Andes* was owned by Cunard and used as a troop transporter & hospital ship in 1854. She was one of the most modern vessels of the day, built in 1852 with a hull constructed of iron and with a screw propeller. *Andes* was returned to transatlantic service in 1855.

[3] (A)Emilius De Vic Tupper – 23rd Regiment - 1st Cousin to TBF, son of Anna Maria (Le Marchant) Tupper and brother of Gaspard & Daniel 'Billy' Tupper.

[4] The project for Dagenham Dock did not evolve further at that time - it was not until approximately 30 years later that the Fanshawe family were able to take advantage of this land acquisition.

I could go on yarning for a long while but am scared of a second summons from the Sergt so with very best love to the Gov, yourself and all of you.

Believe me dearest Mother your most affectionate son

Basil

I was quite struck of a heap at Russell's marriage.

I hope the Governor has got shooting at his place at Upminster. How I should like to join him, there are a few quail here but among the numerous sportsmen, hard to get.

Fancy poor Richard Bayliff's disgust being left at Malta <u>not</u> to come on at present.

Thank the Gov very much for the Illustrated & Punch but we get both, or rather one always sees them. Send this to John – best love to Bab - here is the Sergt!

Goodbye - yesterday was the first time I received a letter on Monday.

Written by Thomas Basil Fanshawe - to his sister, Helen - copied by their mother.
Camp before Sebastopol
September 20th (1855)

My dearest Helen

Neither Edward or yourself must condemn me for not writing as I only received my letters on arriving here this day week when I found a whole heap, not having received any during my absence: in the first place let me thank you both very much for the barrel of beer you have been kind enough to send me by Dick & which I have no doubt we shall enjoy to the uttermost.

Dick has not yet turned up which I fancy must arise from the Russians detention at Constantinople (having shot and shells on board these commodities not being in such demand as formerly). I know Dick was there the beginning of this week as he stopped some fellows of ours on their way up and told them to inform me of his present digging. I shall be very glad to see him again. I was very sorry that I was not present at the last chance at the Redan but as I said in my last, perhaps it is just as well I was not. How pleased the English must be, everyone here hopes it will lead to peace. We have had no end of shaves this week flying about – the latest is that Cronstadt[1] has been taken with a loss of six liners to us and another is that there has been an insurrection in Russia – neither of which I believe but I give them to you as a specimen of how individuals exercise their talents in making and promulgating shaves.

This climate in now getting quite cool a vast difference to Malta - warm things are coming into request and I have written to Aunt

---

[1] Cronstadt or Kronstadt - fortified port in the Baltic guarding St. Petersburg and base of the Russian naval fleet.

Mary by this post to send me up a portmanteau containing the warm things you sent me last February.

I am quite well & jolly now and though we have still only two captains (myself & Ellis) up here our only daily duty is very light. Collings is away sick at Scutari. Our men are employed in making a road to Balaclava and in pulling gabions[1] out of the trenches for fire wood, a much better amusement than putting them up under fire! I have only seen parts of their siege but I hope not to see another. I have not my medal yet but expect at the next distribution to get one, as everyone has a medal and in 9 cases out of 10 with clasps - one will feel rather small – more especially not having or rather not being able to claim anything for Sebastopol. The Light & 2nd Division are not to move at present which is tantamount to saying we shall remain through the winter.

The amount of stores of all kinds taken at Sebastopol is something curious, one thing certain is they never would have fallen short of gunpowder. We have already secured £40,000 worth & at least £80,000 more remain – no end of guns. The Russians are busy making earth works on the North side & firing into the South side, but we fancy they will not remain during the winter, their supplies not being able to reach them. We hear that they are quite staggered at losing the place, never having dreamed it possible - everyone here says our getting it was more luck than anything, also that it was perfect butchery sending the men at the Redan plus the Malakoff was taken - as they swept the whole of the rear of the Redan where they found their men. The Malakoff was the key of the Southside, a great many think a good deal of property is buried in the town & half their powder magazines have not yet been discovered. The town is being pulled to pieces daily by our men buying up daily planks & wood, the flooring gives us capital planks and I am thinking of building a hut for my own use.

---

[1] A basket or cage filled with earth & rocks to support fortifications.

John [xxrythers] came up here the other day, leaving Richard Bayliff at Malta, much to his disgust. I was sorry to find old Gough who led the men at the assault most gallantly died, and also Donovan. Mundy was on the Sea of Azoff, at Kertch[1] & missed it the same as I did. Wickham who was shot in the foot at the attack of the 18th has I hear been just operated upon & I much doubt from what I hear, he can recover the use of his foot. Big Donovan, the Captain is also in a bad way suffering from Erysipelas[2] of the leg coming from the wound in his foot. It is by no means a pleasant thing to look back to what the Regt. was a year ago, & how many are missing & absent now.

But mail is still due, yesterday was the day & I hoped to have found it had brought me letters. I got one from my Mother on Tuesday and I am very sorry to find you have determined on leaving Parsloes, but hope you will be fortunate in the choice of your new residence. I am glad you are not going away immediately – Edward, I am told is shooting with the Govr this year, how I should like to be with them or rather with you all, but of that, I see no chance for the present unless peace is accomplished. I do not think fighting a gentleman's amusement & most are of the same opinion, certainly a siege is not.

I should think you will hardly decipher this if I cross it - with love to Edward, the chicks, the Vicar & Messes believe me dearest Helen

---

[1] An ancient city on the Kerch peninsula in eastern Crimea, situated on the Sea of Asoff (Asov) which by early 19th century had expanded into an important trading and fishing port with an ironwork factory being built in 1846 founded upon the huge iron ore deposits found in the area.

[2] An acute streptococcal infectious disease of the skin, characterized by fever, headache, vomiting, and purplish raised lesions often on the face, legs, toes, arms or fingers. The infection enters the skin through minor trauma, insect bites, dog bites, eczema, athlete's foot, surgical incisions and ulcers, but often originated from strep bacteria in the subject's own nasal passages.

Your most affectionate brother

Basil

Write when you have time, I have not written to John since Constantinople – I suppose he is still with Bab in the country enjoying himself – Tell Edward, the Light Division races come off on the 3 of next month. I will write to him. There are numbers of quail about & I mean to have a turn at them someday, they are very fat & would be a great addition to the table. Anyone in tents is making himself comfortable for the winter. Particularly those who were out last winter and know what it is.

Written by Thomas Basil Fanshawe - to his brother, John Gaspard Fanshawe - copied by their mother.
Camp before Sebastopol
October 5th (1855)

My dearest John

I suppose you received my last from Constantinople and I conclude you have seen and heard from home since then. I got a letter from you last Tuesday - no post mark on it so I presumed it came by a private bag. I am glad to find you are enjoyed your Worcestershire trip – Dick arrived here last Monday and seems greatly pleased with what he has yet seen. I have taken him over the Redan, Sebastopol and the Valley of Death[1] & a few other things, but we have neither of us been in the French batteries or part of the town. D.V.[2] we are going tomorrow.

I did not know till they arrived here of your very kind present of tobacco which will be most acceptable, very many thanks for it. I have not yet got it out of the vessel as the box containing it was stowed away not so handy as the last Fortnum's[3] box from the Gov. I got into camp today & a most glorious supply of eats together with the whisky – I have only the beer to get up, which is a puzzling performance to accomplish on a pack saddle.

---

[1] …'into the Valley of Death rode the six hundred' - from the epic poem 'The Charge of the Light Brigade" written immediately after the Battle of Balaclava in 1854 by the Poet Laureate, Alfred Lord Tennyson.
[2] 'God Willing'.
[3] Established in Duke St. London in 1707, Fortnum & Mason have continuously supplied groceries to fashionable households and soldiers at the front, packaged in their famous hampers. On learning of the plight of the soldiers at the hospitals in Scutari, Queen Victoria sent via Fortnums to Florence Nightingale a huge consignment of concentrated beef tea.

Crimean War Memorial,

Waterloo Place, St. James', London

Matt Benjamin (2016)

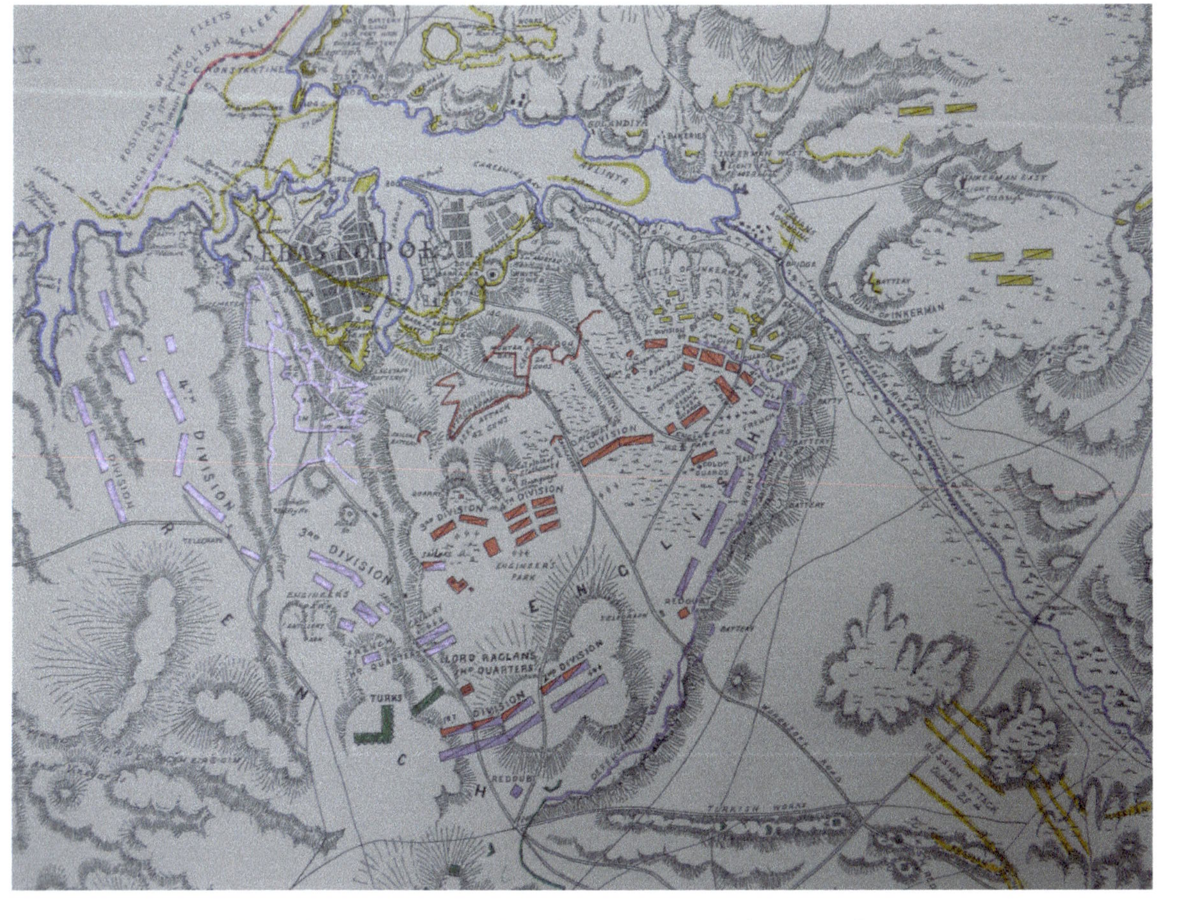

Detail of map showing the camp at Sebastopol
By Roland H Haimes (1986)

I have hardly anything to do now except regimental duty which is very light. Lucky it is too as Ellis and I are the only two captains – Mundy in command came back from Kertch a week after I arrived. Collings is away sick at Scutari & in consequence of poor old Gough's[1] death, will return as Major. Poor G was buried the night before I landed, everyone is sorry for him and also for Donovan. Corbett, from what I hear is not coming back to the Regt.

There is a shave today that the French have turned the Russian left – I hope it may be so. The Russians are very busy on the north side but at present nobody knows if they mean to fight there or evacuate. There will be an awful mess next year if they do not decisively make peace. The Light Cavalry had an order late last night to embark today for Eupatoria but no doubt the latest news will be in the Times. The Light Division races came off last Wednesday, lots of racing such as it was but very great fun as one met nearly everyone out in the Crimea who one knew.

Yesterday's mail brought me no letters but Dick has one from the Govr who I suppose is with the Missus in Guernsey. Many thanks for the Times which since my return has been duly received & before I returned. We are busy in erecting huts, stables etc for the approaching winter. I invested in Gough's horse at his sale last Saturday - £15.10s. & was offered £20 ten minutes afterwards – it was a good strong animal and survived last winter – I don't think I have been stuck.

---

[1] A bachelor and 48 years when he died, Lt. Col. Thomas Bunbury Gough was obviously popular in the 33rd Regiment. His family had a long and exceedingly distinguished military history dating from the 18th century and by the early 20th century three family members had been awarded the Victoria Cross. Another well-decorated soldier was Brigadier Guy Gough DSO, MC. (1893 – 1988) who in retirement explored his family's military heritage and fortunately, he requested the preparation of a map of troop positions during the Crimean War. This original map is shown in this publication by permission of the cartographer, Roland H Haimes.

I hear you have good shooting, how I wish I could have joined you. Give my best love to Bab and the children, which Dick joins. He looks very fresh and well and appears to have enjoyed his trip out extremely. He stopped at Gibraltar, Malta, Constantinople then came aground in the Bosphorus so he has had ample time to see the wonders that he can.

Goodbye for the present. I will write again soon

Dear John, I am your most affectionate brother

Basil

Written by Thomas Basil Fanshawe - to his mother.
Camp Sebastopol
October 12th 1855

My dearest Mother

I was sorry to find by the mail which arrived yesterday and brought me your letter of the 25th of last month that you had not heard from me lately, not knowing of your being away. I wrote to John and also to Helen not thinking that they would be away also. I have written to one of you at least once a week for certain. I am as well and as fresh as a two year old for the trip did me a power of good.

I have very little news to give you. Now that the excitement of trenches is over we are busy making roads and it takes Ellis and myself now alternate duties, having no more captains here, though Collings is due from Scutari but that will be very slight relief and in all probability the next Gazette will bring him his majority through poor Gough's death.

Dick arrived here a week back on Tuesday & seems highly pleased with what he has at present seen. Today I have him so busy on Regimental duty that I have sent him with two of our fellows to see what they think of Inkerman. We were all over the Russian batteries at Sebastopol & he was really under fire, I suppose for the first time, a couple of shots burst somewhere nearby and one fragment came over our heads. The Mamelon, Malakoff, Kamiesh Bay and the monastery[1] are yet to be gone over.

All the things are first rate that he brought out, I have them all stowed away in my tent – many, many thanks from me to the Governor and yourself for your box of tea and the one from Fortnum & Co. I got the beer up all right and everyone who has

---

[1] The Monastery of St Georgia

tasted it pronounced it first rate. Dick got me a lot of crockery from the proprietor of the 'Antelope'[1] who came up to here from Constantinople – Tamplin by name, he came and stayed with me on Saturday last and he went with us into Sebastopol. I also got a sheep for 30/- through him, so my civility was rewarded.

Captain McCrea and his wife (a person whose face I never saw as she always made her appearance at dark) went down from Scutari to Malta in the same ship.

I hope the Governor has recovered from all his bruises in the ribs and arms he got from the steamer, it was very lucky it was not more serious, although a crack of that description is by no means the sort of thing to receive as a reception to the Island or as a farewell to the ship. Next letter, I shall hope to hear of his doing exception amongst the partridges again, how I wish I could join him on his walks. Dick and I went out on Wednesday with a team of the 7th to look for quails around Balaclava which turned out perfect delusion and a snare, as Denison would remark, as we walked from one to four without seeing a bird except an owl which I had a long shot at, peppered but did not get. However we were amply repaid for our struggle up the hills by the view from the top & which I was very glad to show Dick.

I only hope you are enjoying your trip, as much as he appears to be. He looks very fresh & well & still sticks to the razor, rather an uncommon thing out here[2]. Tomorrow night, Dick and I are going to

---

[1] Purchased in 1852 by Millers & Thompson, Liverpool merchants in the Australian trade.

[2] Prior to the war in Crimea, the British army banned beards but due to a shortage of saving soap and the freezing Crimean winter of 1854, soldiers were encouraged to grow their beards for warmth. Based upon the perception that a full beard was the mark of a soldier and hero a fashion soon became established among men of all ages and occupations. This new style was adopted for most of the later decades of the 19th century.

dine with Billy Tupper of the 30th and some more of his Regt who Dick knew at Fermoy[1]. I saw Billy yesterday and in great spirits at the idea of proceeding to England next week which he is nearly certain to do as one of two supernumerary captains with his regiment. Gaspard, I have not seen since my return & Milly[2] only once for a few minutes in Balaclava. The last was filling an Artillery waggon with eatables and drinkables when I left him. Talking of geese, we had a stunner on Tuesday night for dinner, which four of us polished clean off. Dick declares he never had such an appetite as he has here.

By the way the last mail brought him neither 'Illustrated' or 'Punch' which he ordered himself from Pottles[3] at the Exchange. We suppose someone has found it. Rather a nuisance, as poor Donovan who formerly took it in, on his being shot, of course it has been stopped.

Last night a party of 7 of us dined at a Mrs Seacole[4], near Balaclava, who keeps a sort of eating house, it was by no means a comfortable place to dine but the dinner itself was good and the mulled claret after, first rate. We nearly broke our necks, both getting there and home. Dick left our party and went home to the camp of two

---

[1] Fermoy on the River Blackwater in County Cork, site of the largest military barracks in Ireland during the 19th century.

[2] Emilius De Vic Tupper – 23rd Regiment - 1st Cousin to TBF, son of Anna Maria (Le Marchant) Tupper and brother of Gaspard & Daniel 'Billy' Tupper.

[3] Robert Pottle & Son, News Vendors, 14 & 15 Royal Exchange, London.

[4] Mary Jane Seacole (1805 – 1881) a Jamaican-born woman of Scottish and Creole descent who acquired knowledge of herbal medicine in the Caribbean. At the outbreak of the Crimean War she applied to the War Office to go to assist but was refused. Independently she travelled to the front lines and set up a 'British Hotel' behind the lines, described as "a mess-table and comfortable quarters for sick and convalescent officers". She also went out onto the battlefields and gave assistance to wounded soldiers but this valuable work was not officially recognised until 1991 when posthumously she was awarded the Jamaican Order of Merit. In 2004 the British public voted her 'the greatest of all black Britons'.

artillery men who also dined with us. We started from Mrs S together, but having a slight difference which was the nearest way, each party took their own. Dick of course, being perfectly ignorant of the camp let my pony go his own way and reached camp a short time after us.

There is a shave going that the Russians are leaving the Crimea, I only hope it may be true, but they appear very busy on the North side. We are building stables for the winter and some are erecting huts made out of [Sebas Topol]. Peter has a very good one of this material. He talks of going on leave this winter. Did I tell you that Bunbury[1], formerly of ours, who used to be so kind to me, now Lt. Colonel in 23rd is out here? Next camp to ours, but really you would be surprised how little you see of people out of your own camp. Corbett who is away on leave, I hear was to be married on Tuesday last, to a young lady in Berwick, Dickson[2] by name. I knew her when quartered there in '49.

Den wrote by the last mail and seems to be in great spirits and force, he does not say a word about Helen.

I have just heard another shave that the French are on the Belbek but I fancy it is little use telling you shaves as if true you know it long before I could give you. For telegraph, one thing is quite certain, an expedition sailed 7 or 8 days back for somewhere. Some say the (Inxmouth & the Anicsper frigate) is only one man of war before Sebastopol, now the Russians still keep on firing into the town, chiefly on the French but they get as good as they give. Most of the bells[3] which formerly rung in Sebastopol are transferred to the camp

---

[1] Bunbury, Lieutenant-Colonel Henry William C.B. - 23rd Regiment – retired in 1862.

[2] Frank Corbett married Elizabeth Dickson at Berwick-Upon-Tweed on 9th October 1855.

[3] A pair of large bells were taken from the Church of the Twelve Apostles in Sebastopol, each weighing 17cwt 1qr 21lb they were cast by Nicholas Samtoun of

as loot - and generally ring the hours out. In an artillery camp close to us there is a very fine one.

The weather has been rather changeable this last week, rain mixed with a slight dust storm and fine lovely days. I have put Dick in a tent that belongs to one of our people away sick. I had almost forgotten to thank you for the elastic stocking[1] which is just the thing and fits storming. I think I shall have exhausted your patience in deciphering this epistle – unconnected and puzzled together as it is, but I have been so interrupted by fellows coming in, each with something to say. The last informed me he had been killing rats, and the one before him, that lots of fowls were to be at 2/6 each at Kadikoi[2] today. My farm yard now holds a sheep, 5 turkeys, 7 or 8 fowl and three geese with two ducks. Not a bad lot in all.

I shall leave this open till Dick returns, in case he may have a yarn to put in, but he does not seem to like writing here more than at home. We drank all your healths on tapping the beer. Best love to the Governor who I am delighted to hear is so well and the same to yourself.

Believe me, ever dearest Mother, your most affectionate son

Basil
I shall write to John next week, so you may send this on or not as you like.

Moscow. In February 1856, these war trophies were displayed at the Woolwich Royal Arsenal. When the Cambridge Military Hospital at Aldershot was built in 1879, one bell was hung in the hospital's clock tower. The second of the pair was installed at Windsor Castle and called the Sebastopol Bell it is still tolled at great solemn state occasions.

[1] The first elastic stockings were based on the invention of vulcanized rubber by Charles Goodyear of America in 1839 coupled with circular knitting machine invented by Marc Isambard Brunel.

[2] A village 1 mile north of Balaclava.

Written by Thomas Basil Fanshawe - to his mother - copied by their mother.

[Note on top left corner of letter]
I forget the No. of my last letter so shall number this 10

Camp Sebastopol
October 22th (1855)

My dearest Mother

The mail today brought no letters or papers either for Dick or I but on Friday last we got your letter & papers. Many thanks, I was at drill the whole morning & till late in afternoon President of a Ct Martial so Dick said he would write, which he did to Bab & I suppose they sent it to you by this.

Since last Wednesday the whole army is under arms at daylight, which is anything but pleasant these cold mornings. Thursday, Friday and Saturday last the whole of the Light Division was kept off duty for drill & we were at it the whole day. I believe the reason why we turn out so early is that General Simpson got a telegraph message from England, stating that the Russians were going to attack us, in fact a sort of 2nd Inkerman was expected & Saturday & Sunday last were the days prophesied by the knowing ones, as being the day fixed for the fight, but I hardly think that the Ruskies will attack us. At any rate they will find us prepared & I think now that the moon is up nearly all night, they will give the idea up, as they cannot get their men into position without being seen.

I need not say, Master Dick does not turn out at these early hours & does not half like the early hour at which we retire at night – ten o/c at the latest. Since we have then turned out at 5, I generally go to bed again for a couple of hours.

Tuesday night last I spent at Fort Paul on picquet[1], the Russians treated us very civilly as they only fired a round shot at us just as we got there, which went over our heads. I was with 50 men & 1 subaltern to look out in case the Russians took it into their heads to pay a visit from the other side, but nothing stirred in the harbour. I got back to camp about 8 o/c, went to sleep till 10 o/c & then went down to the Balaclava plain to see the Cavalry races. I cannot say much for the races but we met no end of a lot of people one knows.

I forgot to say that Billy Tupper dined with Dick here on Tuesday night, but of course being at Fort Paul, they missed my pleasing society. Billy went away for England on Saturday last, in great spirits. Gaspard, I have not yet seen & Milly only once since May last.

We heard on Friday that the Forts at Kinburn[2] had been taken and today there is a shave that the Fleet have been bombarding Odessa, the bombardment to last three days, so the Ruskies are getting the agony piled on pretty stiff, one way & another. Dick and I were over the Mamelon & Malakoff yesterday. They are curious old diggings & the explosion in the first, of which we saw the remains, must have been awful & the French, I cannot help thinking that they lost more than they owned to. We had a good look at the Russians on the other side, they did not appear to be so busy as usual, not in such numbers. I wish if they are going, "they would not stand on the order of their going", but hook it at once & leave us Sebastopol to winter in. I have not found it cold yet, except early in the morning which of course is the coldest time.

---

[1] A small temporary military post closer to the enemy than the main formation.
[2] The French & British Navy took the Forts during the Battle of Kinburn (or Kil-Bouroun) on 17th October 1855 when ironclad warships were first brought into use. The forts were taken within 4 hours, proving that the ships could withstand heavy Russian fire with minimal casualties and achieve the objective quickly.

I have written down to Malta for a portmanteau which I left there. I heard from Aunt Mary a short time back - all well. Eleanor, not yet made her appearance. Tell John, Dick and I dined with Tom Pakenham, 30th on Wednesday, he is very fresh and all right again. I think I have told you all about our proceedings since my last & hope you will not be tired at reading so much about ourselves. Many thanks for the flannels which I have no doubt will prove most useful. I was very glad to find that both the Governor and yourself are so fresh & well & enjoyed your trip to Guernsey. John tells me in his last that Helen was in trouble with her servants but by this time I hope they are over, as well as my fears about you and the ague.

Young Tupper[1] of the 23rd has gone home seriously wounded in the foot & Drs seem to think that he will be very lucky if he saves his foot.

I hope you did not suffer from walking into the pond, will you give the enclosed to Sockett[2], just a line to thank him for some cigars.

Dick today went to see a French review which I have since heard did not come off. He has not yet returned, I could not go, being on Ct Martial, as usual – always am on a mail day. Dick picked up a few mementos from the Mamelon and Malakoff and all of us brought away lots of fleas, which abound there. Dirty devils those Russians must be.

Collings came back last Monday, we are trying to get up a mess & hope to succeed. I cannot tell you how much I appreciate the

---

[1] Lt. Daniel Tupper – sent down to the Depot on 16 October 1855 before being transported home.

[2] A near neighbour of Dagenham Vicarage & member of the Vestry (early form of Parish Council) - Richard Sockett of Rookery Farm, Dagenham having 206 acres employing 8 labourers and 4 boys (1861 Census).

contents of the box from Fortnums - Dick will be able to tell you on his return I suppose - about Xmas you will see him, he seems to enjoy this sort of life.

Best love to the Gov., Helen, Edward and the same to yourself in which Dick joins.

Believe me ever dearest Mother, your most affectionate son

Basil

Dick wrote to ~~John~~ Bab on Friday, so I thought it was no use sending duplicates. The Assistant Quarter Master General of Eyre's brigade is vacant and no one will take the appointment he is such a beast.

Written by Thomas Basil Fanshawe - to his brother, John Gaspard
Fanshawe - copied by their mother.
Camp before Sebastopol
November 2nd (1855)

My dearest John,

Dick having written to Bab so very lately I have delayed writing
especially at this dull time.

We have been most fortunate in our weather which has been lovely,
we have been pretty well worked, in particularly the men making
roads preparing for the winter but I am glad to see we have not
much more work to do in this line. When in camp I have been
overlooking my servants erecting a kitchen. Our men are so busy I
cannot build both a kitchen & a hut and as I have a double tent &
have driven musket barrels into the ground instead of tent pegs, I
am not in much fear of coming to grief this winter.

The dust has been awful yesterday & today – yesterday I was out
road making & nearly blinded by it. I am on again tomorrow, we
have to march away from the parade ground at 7am and do not get
back till 4pm. It is rather monotonous but much superior to trench
work.

Last Sunday morning, I am glad to say was the last of our daybreak
parades, we are not a little delighted at their having come to an end.
The Russians keep on firing from the North side but with little
effect. There have been one or two short explosions from men
treading on fougasses[1], but not much harm done. There is nearly

---

[1] 'a series of small mines or barrels of gunpowder let into the ground between our
works and theirs, and a little tin tube running along the ground a few inches above
it, two or three feet long, which tube is filled with some composition which
explodes immediately on being touched, so that any unfortunate meandering along

nothing going on worth writing about, Dick and I rode over on Friday last to the Monastery, we heard the monks perform their service, not a long one. It is a very pretty place and we could easily have passed 3 or 4 more hours there, but we wanted to get back by daylight. You have no idea what work it is finding your way to a distant camp in the dark, even if you know your way. Three times in going, I lost my way in going to dine with Milly Tupper on Monday with Dick – returning we had no difficulty for the moon was up.

Yesterday I was rather seedy from the old thing but I stopped it at once & am all right again. Tom Pakenham, I come across now and then, he is very much better than he was on arriving.

I hope you have been having good shoot this year, there are some woodcock to be got near Baidai, but I really have not had time to go anywhere lately, all this week I have been trying to go to Kamiesh with Dick but each day something has turned up to stop us. Dick talks of taking his departure next week, I shall be very sorry when he goes and do not see why he need start so early. He is trying hard to get some Russian trophies but they are very difficult to obtain now. Carr got the best I have yet seen – a silver cross, about 10 inches long with medallions of saints on it, he gave a guard £4 for it & has since been offered 20 – He has sent an application to go home this winter but it is very uncertain if he gets it, both he and his brother are flourishing.

Helen and Edward wrote by last mail, they wrote in good spirits. By the time this reaches England I suppose you will be settled again in Chester Terrace – I am glad to see by your last that Bab has

---

the grass without knowing why, suddenly finds himself going up in the air like a squib with his legs and arms flying in different directions. We have had many men blown up by these things and the grass being so long one cannot see the tube at all. The technical name is Fougasse'. *Extract from the Cheshire Archives – Letters of Colonel Hugh Robert Hibbert (1828 – 1895).*

benefited by her visit in the country, also the chick. Has Bab's brother[1] in the 48th any chance of coming out? I shall soon hear of his arrival as Williamson[2] is in them, and still here. He made many enquiries after you the other day. He is covered with jet black hair & very little altered in manner. There was a letter in the Naval & Military Gazette[3] a short time back pitching into Tom Coventry for getting his company over the heads of his seniors, did you see the letter? I do not suppose he felt it severely. This mail which we hourly expect will bring the Gazette containing the promotions for the taking of Sebastopol, also poor old Gough's vacancy - that will leave Ellis and me for duty. Corbett's brother came here two days ago *en amatear* he says his brother <u>had sent in his papers to sell,</u> Ellis says he has <u>not,</u> which is the one to be believed? Perhaps he has changed his mind again. I should be sorry to see him leave the Regiment though he is my senior. Mundy, if one can believe him, says he has written for Lay to join his regt. This will rather touch him up and I should not be surprised if he exchanged.

The flies here are not quite as bad as they were in the summer and the mice get everything not kept in tins, I wish I knew how to destroy the brutes - there are no [indeere] traps here. I shall have to resort to the old plan of cracking them with a brick, the practice of gardeners. Tonight I am going to dine with General Codrington who commands our division, the first time he has asked me. I hear he gives a capital dinner.

I have just returned from the General's, had an excellent dinner & and heard a variety of reports which I will relate to you: <u>First </u>that the Russians are going to attack us either on the 6 or 7 or 8 which

---

[1] John Willoughby Coventry (1837 -1905) - an officer in the 48th & 15th Regiments - brother of Barbara 'Bab' Coventry, wife of John Gaspard Fanshawe.
[2] Major W. R. Williamson - The Northamptonshire Regiment (48th).
[3] The Naval & Military Gazette and Weekly Chronicle of the United Service (published 1833 to 1886) incorporated into The Broad Arrow: A Paper for the Services London.

means I suppose that we shall have daybreak parades for more days, they will get an awful licking. The quarantine fort blew up the other day, no lives lost, caused by the decomposition of some filth. The Docks are going to be dredged. There is a good story about a man Buckmaster my tailor. Sent out for orders, it seems this gent was found drunk in Balaclava in the street, he was caught by the Provost Martial[1] who had him up & gave him two dozen lashes well laid on. His recollection of the Crimea will be <u>feeling</u>, I should think when he recalls his travels.

The Russians have got an enormous watch fire burning tonight, looks as if it covered more than a mile beyond the Tchenaya.

General Eyre's staff is, I hear terrible to be on, he charges them like a pick pocket. I am on a working party tomorrow & have to be up early so shall conclude with much love to Bab, the chick in which Dick joins. I have not seen your handwriting for more than 3 weeks. I hope soon to hear from you. Tell my Mother with my love, I received the shirts etc all right by M Tupper – I am much obliged. Our mail was late by the French boat at Marseilles[2] so we shall have here no letters or papers till Monday – pleasant night after very frigid this morning -

Believe me you affectionate brother

Basil

---

[1] During the Crimean War, a Mounted Staff Corps of almost 100 troopers from the Police Constabulary of Ireland, with some recruited from London's Metropolitan Police, was established to prevent the theft of supplies and maintain discipline in camps. The 'Corps' was disbanded after the cessation of hostilities.

[2] According to GPO Notice 23 - 22 May 1854, mail was transported by French packet from Constantinople via Marseilles to Southampton and return, 6 times a month. In December that year it was increased to twice a week.

Written by Thomas Basil Fanshawe - to his mother - copied by his mother.
Camp before Sebastopol
November 16th (1855)

My dearest Mother

Yesterday Dick left this to go on board the 'Bachaute' in which he got a passage down to Scutari. I am sorry to say I could not go down to the vessel with him being on Court Martial, I got away about a ¼ to 1o'clock and rode down from our camp sharp to try and catch the ship before she started, but was too late. I did say good bye to him before he left camp in the morning, but I made certain I should see him again. He talks of going home by Smyrna[1] and Cairo & in all probability will have a look at the Pyramids. This arrangement depends on him catching one of Cunard's[2] boats at Constantinople which takes this route. It will be very jolly if he can manage it, in this case he will I think have <u>done</u> the East pretty well. He enjoyed himself very much and was fortunate enough to pick up a variety of trophies which will adorn his room among the other curiosities hold a conspicuous place.

Coming home yesterday about 3½ o'clock, just after passing Kadikoi I witnessed a most grand but awful sight which no doubt you have already heard of through the telegraph. The explosion of the French right siege train close to our camp, indeed not two minutes' walk from it. I was riding quietly when a flash struck across the sky & caught my attention. Looking in the direction I saw a faint pink light for about half a mile, this was followed by a mess or rather a pillar

---

[1] An ancient city situated at a strategic point on the Aegean coast today called İzmir, Turkey.
[2] During the Crimean War Cunard supplied 11 ships for war service when every British North Atlantic route was suspended until 1856 except Cunard's Liverpool-Halifax-Boston service.

of dark grey coloured smoke rising perpendicularly to the height of about ½ a mile – when it appeared to burst open, shells and rockets showered out of the smoke in every possible quarter of the heavens. This report was awful – my description is very poor but the whole thing was so momentary, there was but little time for observation. I was 6 or 7 miles from the scene & at first could not make out what it was, but on arriving at the top of the hill someone told me what had happened.

I galloped on fearing to find the regiment almost destroyed, in fact the division. We had a party of 1 captain & subaltern & 150 men working on the roads close by. Wonderful to say, actual loss of the divisions and regiment is slight when you think of 50 tons of powder exploding which I believe is the amount lost. The Division has lost 68 killed & wounded but it is difficult to find out the numbers correctly. The Regt only lost 2 men killed & 13 wounded, no officer touched.

I hear the accident arose from a French soldier pricking a loaded shell which was lying loose with his bayonet and which went off & communicated to the magazine in succession. This is only (a) report and I cannot vouch for the truth of it but Artillery have lost 52 men killed and wounded. What about the French loss it has not yet been heard, some say 40 but it must be much more. The poor fellows who were killed yesterday are now being buried. Our siege train has no powder, it is separated only by the road from the French siege train but quantities of shells & combustibles are being piled together. Our powder magazine is an old windmill which you may have seen depicted in the 'Illustrated Times'. It is about 200 yards from the siege train and contained 8 hundred thousand crates of ammunition of different descriptions or about 150 tons of powder and if this had been ignited by a shell (of which there was every chance) no one would have been alive to tell the tale. Of course, every hut & building near the train is destroyed.

We were all turned out & almost all our men except 40 were employed in wetting blankets & fastening them around the mill, a nice occupation not knowing how soon you might be blown up either by the mill exploding or a bit of shell. I got to camp about 7 o'clock, turned out with the men who went down to the Victoria Redoubt. The men did not come back to camp till the fire was nearly out & all safe – about 7 o'clock. Our mess hut was smashed in ~~at one end, 4 fellows~~ by a piece of shell, 4 fellows were in it at the time - no one hurt. Almost all our men's huts were much shaken, my tent stood all right, thanks to the iron gun barrels & a piece of the bannister found in ~~Sebastopol~~ the barracks at Sebastopol, for a tent pole. We turned out this morning at 5 o'clock, in case the Russians got bumptious at the explosion and thought to find us in confusion. I need scarcely say <u>they</u> did not turn out to attack us. I have just heard the following list of casualties is correct: English - 1 Commissariat[1] officer killed, 1 Artillery officer lost a foot, 20 men killed and 141 wounded. French loss about 400 – I hear also the explosion was caused by the French carrying powder loose from one magazine to the other in a careless way (men no doubt smoking).

Have you seen that Corbett has left us – by this I am in the same position as if I had purchased my company in 1854 - Carr has got his company and appeared in general orders yesterday for leave to England but the Colonel has endeavoured to stop him as he went this morning. If he goes, Prescott & myself are the only two captains for duty - a pleasant prospect for the winter.

The mail today brought me a letter from you, many thanks I am sorry to find John was so unwell but hope by this time he is all right again. He must have suffered much, carbuncles[2] are I understand so

---

[1] Land Transport Corps formed 1855, renamed the Military Train the following year and later Royal Army Service Corps.

[2] Inflammatory skin condition - a multi-headed pus-filled boil infected by the germ Staphylococcus. Extremely painful and possibly life threatening, the treatment

painful. Dick wrote to you last week while I was on guard on the Karabelnaia[1]. The guard is just before you get into Sebastopol Dockyard, having the white barracks in front of you & the Redan in rear. The Russians were very quiet and only fired 7 shots while I was there, none very near us. The duty now is busy what with road making, Court Martials - but anything is better than the trenches.

My kitchen walls stood the explosion well but a bit of shell came through the roof and smashed a couple of rafters, but the damage is easily repaired. Our weather is beautiful still, but beginning to get sharp frost latterly – wonderful weather. Two days ago I received my portmanteau from Malta and wore the red polka Helen made me this morning. I found it most comfortable. I am sorry to say the moths have got into the portmanteau and played old boots with some fur things there. I have heard from Eleanor who gives no news but says Aunt Mary is anything but well. The red flannel[2] you were kind enough to send me from Guernsey has not yet turned up, but no doubt in time it will. I much doubt my seeing Branfill[3] of the 10th Hussars for some time, I have no time even to look Gaspard up & when I go down to Balaclava it is generally on business for the

---

before modern antibiotics relied upon the application of hot poultices, lancing and cleaning with hydrogen peroxide.

[1] On the Inkerman side at the foot of line of defences the harbour formed from the inland River Tchernaya and a road and viaduct led into the Karabelnaia, round the head of the Carreen Bay.

[2] Red flannel - a cholera belt, usually a flat strip of flannel (mostly red) or knitted wool about six feet long and six inches wide, worn as a precautionary measure against chills to the abdomen, the belts were often standard Army issue in cold and tropical climates. Outbreaks of cholera and dysentery were greatly feared in all densely populated areas and even into the early 20th century cholera belts or cummerbunds were still in use.

[3] Benjamin Aylett Branfill (1828–1899) 10th Hussars – later Lt. Col of the regiment and Deputy Asst. Q.M General in Ireland - his family lived at Upminster Hall, approximately 5 miles from Parsloes. He inherited the property in 1873 but not long after travelled to Nelson in New Zealand and settled. There he became known as a talented artist exhibiting at the NZ Academy of Fine Art in Wellington.

larder. Time slips away wonderfully fast hunting about shops these short days.

I conclude the Govr & yourself are flourishing as you say nothing about yourselves. Goodbye for the moment – if I can I will write more but that is doubtful - so with best love to all

Believe me ever dearest Mother – your very affectionate son

Basil

Written by Thomas Basil Fanshawe - to his mother.
Camp Sebastopol
Saturday December 1st 1855

My dearest Mother

Many thanks for your last two letters, the mail today brought me your last of the 16th Nov. I am sorry to find that John still continues seedy, but I hope that he is right by this - I am glad to hear he got my last letter as in his last he seemed to think I had been rather slack lately. I have written to him by this post.

I am in robust health although the weather has completely altered the last ten days – rain, snow, sleet & frost have followed in quick succession and our camp is mud up to the ankles – about as much as the men's tent inside last winter had and gives one a faint idea of what misery the men had to undergo at that period last winter. But thank God we have no trenches and for nearly 3 weeks now I have not been on guard or picquet, but court martials. I expect it is heading to my turn round and it is no joke passing these long nights on a Fort Pascal picquet 27 hours on the Karabelnaia guard however I am pretty well off for warm clothing & waterproof, having coats, trousers, caps and gloves of the better material which Dick was kind enough to leave me. The young [rip] has now left here a fortnight & have not had a line from him so I expect he has cut the Cairo boat off. I told John I just missed seeing him off.

I have been obliged to leave my tent, as it was in the way to the officer's hut which is in the course of erection, but unfortunately it has been most carelessly finished by the contractor at home & we have to do his work. I fancy it will not be over comfortable but it is better than a tent as till you have practicable demonstration, the nuisance of getting into a tent on a wet and windy night is not to be supposed. You dare not undo the canvas opening, as how is to be shut – but Dick will put you up to a wrinkle as to campaigning – much better than a demonstration by letter. Our mess hut is still in exactly the same state as it was in from after the explosion, thanks to our Commanding Officer Lt. Col. Mundy who has not taken the slightest trouble about it – ask why? He has got a very comfortable sandstone house of his own and he comes swaggering in after a heavy rain or snow storm with some such explanation as this " By Jove, I thought you fellows would have had the hut down last night, I do not think it will stand another" – pleasant this! I am writing in it now (8 o'clock Friday evening – by the way I always date my letters a day previous to the mail leaving, this time I have not) – and having no door except an old blanket which I myself got nailed up, the sound which is by no means of the sort to come under the head of gentle breezes is more airy than agreeable to the legs and the candle flickers in a most unsteady way. My kitchen is only down about three feet into the earth, a sort of small potato clamp then over this fits a wall composed of mud mixed with lime & stones, it is then covered with a wooden roof, sloping, & this is again covered with an old tent & only wants a few gallons of tar to make it completely waterproof.

You seem to think that I did not look after No 1 in building this before a home for myself, but now I am certain of always getting my grub all right & I have a right to use strong language if it is not forthcoming. It is not such a green trick as you think, besides if the worst comes to the worst I can do in a double tent well enough as I should build a fireplace and make myself as jolly as possible. The only thing against the tent being the entrance, as I said on the other page - we really should have nothing to complain of had we our house up and mess hut in order. I trust by this day week to be able to give you a line that such is the case.

You will be glad to hear that all the men of my company (the Light) are in two huts & really watertight, a great contrast to this time last year. They are all served out with a long pair of boots up to the knees, jerseys, drawers, comforters etc & very comfortable. My men have been going on well, not very much drunkenness, but two men in the Regt. died drunk or rather from the effects of liquor a short time back, an awful thing to think off.

What do you suppose? My company is in credit! That is money that they can draw any moment, over £200 & I generally have to send home about 30 pounds a month from them but it is very hard to persuade the British soldier to think that he is not being done in sending remittances home & he very naturally argues "I get so much a day for fighting, I have got nothing from my friends & next spring or next guard or picquet I go on, I may get nibbed out. Why not enjoy it while I can?" Of course it is the reasoning of an untaught man, but it is hard to show him cause to the contrary.

I am glad to say our Regt has been going on much better latterly. Today's post brought word that Colonel Johnstone is coming out to join us. That imposter & I am going to say <u>liar,</u> Mundy on hearing the intelligence, declared he would start for England tomorrow: all this is Bosh[1] and Mundy will be here till duly relieved, of course this is private. His game is to get away before the spring campaign commences, it will be no trifling matter when we move, which report says is to be about the end of March. I expect next year to be a Regt Major if I live, certainly a Brevet Major & had I been present, should have got the latter rank for Sebastopol! However I do not grumble. I am glad to say that I get the Sebastopol Clasp & think I am quite as much entitled to it as the cavalry who never did a days, or an hour's duty in the trenches since landing. What do you think?

I wonder how young Bramfill manages so badly, rations well-cooked are not to be despised. I do not use the salt rations as on account of drink which is expensive. Pretyman I think will get a

---

[1] empty or meaningless talk or opinions; nonsense (C19: from Turkish *boş* empty).

good staff appointment, Wickham I doubt re-joining, Ellis has had enough fighting, being a married, would go if he can do it decently & Donovan is in a bad way, I fancy. I do [not] see why I should not be a major shortly, it is all luck.

From old fish, Going is hanging on so long – I am glad to hear such good accounts of the dock company[1], I trust it will turn out better than you expect. How glad I am to hear that the Governor is so fresh, you seem to have had colder weather than us, although the Hills are covered with snow. I have a cold bath every morning & uncommon cold the water gets.

I hope the Governor's post will delight my eyes soon, fancy next Monday is my birthday – how I should like to be under the old roof again. However let us hope we may meet sooner than we expect.
Your fernery[2], I am glad to hear is so flourishing. I got when on guard in Sebastopol some Convululus Major[3] seeds which I duly gave to Dick to deliver & I hope to see it growing on my return. It comes from the Karabelnaia Suburb. I should think that you would have enough to give Helen some.

---

[1] During 1855 the well-known engineer Sir John Rennie was working to convert Dagenham Breach into a wet dock, but he ran out of money. The Breach was a large lake which had been formed in the 17th century by the River Thames breaking through the protective river wall. It was another 30 years before the docks were developed and a connecting railway to London began the process of turning Dagenham's riverside into an industrial area of national significance.

[2] Fernery - a collection of ferns, displayed and cultivated either in a conservatory or outside in a shady dell. During 1855 many people in England were gripped by 'the fern craze' or 'pteridomania' as it was called by Charles Kingsley, a naturalist and clergyman who later wrote The Water Babies. Collections included both British and foreign types of fern, and presumeably with two sons travelling beyond western Europe, Katherine Fanshawe hoped to enlarge and improve her new fernery at Dagenham's Vicarage.

[3] Convolvulus Purpureus Purple Bindweed or Convolvulus Major - an annual plant growing naturally in Asia and America. With trumpet shaped flowers, it is cultivated in English gardens in white, purple and red & white varieties.

Many thanks for the last which I will answer soon, but I really have nothing to communicate and although this epistle may frighten you I doubt it being very interesting. Many thanks for asking what would be most useful, really I know nothing I want except some of 'The Times' now and then, not that they are of much use to me as the Mess takes in lots of papers, but my men appreciate a late 'Times' and so if you can manage it without trouble, I shall be much obliged.

I must have a warm at the fire before I go to bed, so with best love to the Governor, has he had any shooting lately? – Helen, Edward and their chicks at Parsloes – and the same to yourself.

Believe me, ever dearest Mother, your most affectionate son

Basil

Written by Thomas Basil Fanshawe - to his mother.
Camp Sebastopol
Friday December 7th (1855)

My dearest Mother

The mail today brought me your last of November 21st many thanks. I am writing this in my old place, the mess hut & the candle as usual flickering like blazes, so you must make allowances for any irregularity which may occur. I have nothing much to tell you since writing this day week.

Here is my diary –
Saturday - rain hard with high wind working at officer's hut.
Sunday - parade which was shortened by a snow storm, worked at hut for remainder of day, several hail storms, dined out.
Monday - went to races between Kamiesh & monastery, great fun - steeple chasing the order of the day, lots of falls, no damage done. Pelissier[1] and Codrington both present & hardly anything but officers present. Got a letter from John.
Tuesday - nothing particular going on, reading papers brought by mail yesterday and the periodicals our Mess take in.
Wednesday - on the roads i.e. making them, but got off early as the men were given a piece of road and the sooner they did it, the sooner they got home. Consequently, I got to camp again about 12 o/c – awfully cold, all having to parade at 6 o/c in the morning instead of 7.30, a great nuisance in a dark morning - had frost in the morning which turned to rain, in bed at 10 o/c.

---

[1] Aimable-Jean-Jacques Pélissier, 1st Duc de Malakoff (1794 - 1864) Marshal of France was appointed Commander-in-chief of the French forces during May 1855, before the Siege of Sebastopol. Determined to conduct the campaign without interference from Paris, he succeeded in the storming of the Tower of Malakoff on 8 September and ended the Siege of Sebastopol.

'Council of War held at Lord Raglan's head quarters, the morning of
The successful attack on the Mamelon. Lord Raglan, Marechal Pelissier & Omar Pacha'
Roger Fenton, 1855 - Library of Congress

'Lieutenant General Sir William J. Codrington K.C.B.'

Roger Fenton, (1855) - Library of Congress

'General Sir James Simpson, G.C.B.'

Roger Fenton, (1855) - Library of Congress

'Lieutenant General Sir George Brown G.C.B. & Officers of his staff,
Major Hallewell, Colonel Brownrigg, orderly, Colonel Airey, Captain Pearson,
Captain Markham, Captain Ponsonby'

Roger Fenton, (1855) - Library of Congress

'Private in full marching order'

Roger Fenton, (1855) - Library of Congress

Charles van Straubenzee

Felice Beato, (1858 - 1859) - Wikimedia Commons

Edmund Lyons

Engraving by D. J. Pound (1857) - Wikimedia Commons

Thursday - rain like blazes, thought my tent was coming down from the force of the wind - rode into Balaclava on a foraging cruise (geese, ducks etc.) but beyond lunching on board the 'Andes' which brought me out, did nothing.

Today - on a Ct martial tried three prisoners & rest of the afternoon, busy in ~~afternoon~~ dividing the partitions of the officer's hut. Thank providence I have got a compartment to myself which I mean to go into tomorrow. I have dug two holes in the ground & lit two fires there to dry the ground & mean to make myself comfortable.

I have given you the last week's summary & now to answer your numerous queries. You have by this received my account of the explosion etc., I wrote the next day. Dick saw it, as I learnt yesterday from the steward of the 'Bacchaute', but I suppose he is with you by this. How I wish I could be with you for your Xmas gathering. The stores you mention as being destroyed by Sir E Lyons,[1] could not be brought here or you may depend they would. I wrote to Eleanor 3 weeks ago, but have received no answer yet, too soon. I always write when I get an answer to my last as you know is my way.

This mail, I heard from John. I was sorry to find that he was not quite the thing yet and bothered by the servants. I hope your visit to Chobham[2] was a pleasant one and the Govr had good shoot with the snipe the second day. An old poacher is generally good company - how I wish I could have had a turn at the snipe in the Govr's

---

[1] Admiral Edmund Lyons, 1st Baron Lyons, GCB, KCH (1790 – 1858), a retired distinguished RN commander who later held various ambassadorial posts in Sweden, Switzerland and Greece before being persuaded back into the Royal Navy as Commander of the Black Sea Fleet.

[2] Chobham Place, the home of Sir Denis Le Marchant, 1st Baronet (1795 – 1874), eldest brother of TBF's mother. A barrister, civil servant, writer and MP, he held ministerial posts in Whig governments and from 1850 until 1871 held the permanent post of Clerk of the House of Commons.

society[1]. Sir E Colebrook[2] and G LeFevre[3] I never saw, they left I think, before I came back from Malta.

I regret to say that my correspondence with Halifax is limited, but I have nowadays so little to say that I am afraid of writing a stupid epistle. I hope Johnny's[4] leg will get right eventually. The mud in camp is up to our ankles. I wear India rubber boots[5] which Sir Gaspard gave me before leaving Halifax, they are better than most things, their only drawback being their retaining the perspiration which makes your feet cold. Occasionally we have a quiet drink, but generally in bed by twelve & unless for duty, breakfast between 9 & 10.

I am sorry to find that Mr Allen's proposal for the living has not succeeded but let us hope it may turn out all right. Young Bramfill as I told you last week, I have not seen. I think the Regt have either gone or going to the Bosphorus for the winter, where I hope he will find himself more comfortable. My dinner today was a soup-like mutton broth, fish from Balaclava, mutton chops and cheese which you sent out. Many thanks for it. Tomorrow I have the remainder of the ham for breakfast – the first has been consumed. Dinner today was an average specimen but not what I call the best of produce. My

---

[1] The Governor's companions at this shoot, Sir Denis Le Marchant, Sir Edward Colebrooke & Sir John Shaw Lefevre were all educated at Eton & Cambridge.

[2] Sir (Thomas) Edward Colebrooke, 4th Baronet (1813 – 1890) MP for Taunton 1842–1852, Lanarkshire 1857–1868 and North Lanarkshire 1868–1885. He was also Lord Lieutenant of Lanarkshire 1869–1890.

[3] Sir John George Shaw-Lefevre KCB (1797 –1879) brother-in-law of Sir Denis Le Marchant: British barrister, Whig politician and civil servant, between 1856 and 1875 served as Clerk of the Parliaments. He helped found the University of London, serving as Vice-Chancellor for many years and for his services to the public was made KCB in 1857.

[4] John Le Marchant – 1st cousin of TBF.

[5] In 1855, Charles Goodyear from USA challenged the English manufacturer Hancock in a patent dispute - it may be that TBF owned one of the first pairs of rubber 'wellies'?

geese are first rate & fat as possible, I wish you could have partaken of our last. I assure you it would not have disgraced your table and you were sure to get a good one of the species.

Remember me to Charlotte and Mrs Bramfill, I should think her son, if he did not inform the professors that he had a palate, or rather no palate, would get a commission. Young Seymour[1], 68 – I occasionally see, he was in good spirits but how he gets on in his Regt I do not know. It is a good corps & I have no doubt gets on well. I should fancy he holds his own pretty well.

I presume this will reach you by about Xmas day. How I wish I could join your party. If you think this is worth showing to John, send it with a Merry Xmas and Happy New Year to all at Parsloes, the Vicarage & Chester Terrace[2]. Dick will give you some wonderful yarns.

I must close this what I am afraid will be a stupid epistle, with best love to the Gov & yourself, ever dearest Mother

Your most affectionate son

Basil

---

[1] Seymour Le Marchant - 68th Regiment - 1st cousin of TBF and son of Sir John Gaspard Le Marchant, Lt-Governor of Nova Scotia.
[2] 22 Chester Terrace, Eaton Square, the first marital home of John Gaspard & Barbara Fanshawe.

Tell John with many thanks, that I got his letter & Letts[1] diary. One epistle is quite enough to inflict on the family. Peter is within a yard of me and desires kind remembrances. The weather is most changeable, cannot depend on it more than 12 hours together, it was a most beautiful sunset tonight but very likely rain will fall tomorrow morning.

---

[1] John Letts, bookbinder & printer of the Royal Exchange published the first commercially produced diary in 1816 as Letts Diary or Bills Owed Book and Almanac. His son Thomas (1803-1873) developed the business and annually published many different types & sizes of diaries which were exceeding fashionable and popular and has remained so until the present day.

Written by Thomas Basil Fanshawe - to his brother, John Gaspard Fanshawe - copied by his mother.
Camp before Sebastopol
December 17th (1855)

My dearest John

I cannot let another post go out without giving you a line although I am afraid this will be anything but a lively letter. I suppose this will reach you sometime between Xmas and New Year's Day. I hope you and Bab will have had a merry Xmas and are looking forward to a happy new year; how I wish I could join you, let us hope next year we shall be altogether again. Everyone here hopes that a peace may be squared before the Spring - too good to come to pass, I doubt.

Our mail has been due since Thursday & no sign of its arrival yet - our post day has changed, the letters going on Monday & Friday nights.

By this time I hope that you are quite recovered from the effects of the carbuncles.

During the last week we have had some freezing frosts & last night it began to snow & so continues today in occasional showers. I have left my tent & am installed in the big hut. I have a compartment to myself & find it a great improvement to a tent, not so much chance of being blown out at night which now and then happens even in the hut. The hut is anything but sultry, although I have a stove in my place it is hardly sufficient to warm the room. I am writing in it now, my fingers are so cold you must excuse the badness of the writing.

Among other things that are new since I wrote last is an untiring picquet of a company per regiment, you parade at 9 and have to remain in camp ready to turn out if wanted. The worst part is having to be under arms at reveille, beating which is at 5 o'clock. I was out this morning and was very glad to get in again. I lit a fire, made some chocolate & turned in again - as this only comes around about once every 8 days, it is not very hard work.

Of late we have had very little drunkenness as military prisons have been established which the men do not approve of at all.

This day week we had steeple chasing between Kameish and the Monastery, great fun. The day was fine & all the races were good and although plenty of croppers, no-one was hurt. Codrington and Palissier were both present & numerous other great people. At night there was a great dinner at a restaurant just behind the 4th Division. I was asked but did not go – about 70 sat down. In the course of the evening they drank the health of the writers who were in the Crimea – Russell[1] (Times Correspondent) returned thanks & let out he was going away. When he had finished (Astley) got up and in his stagey style, chased him for the remarks he had made on officers going on leave. I hear it was capitally done.

I forgot to thank you for Letts diary which arrived 10 days back with your letter. Last Thursday I rode down to Kemiesh with one of our fellows to get some things for the hut, had lunch there - what do you think they ask for a woodcock – 12 francs!! I have passed most of my time in camp, there is no inducement to go out besides the last week I have been busy at work on the officer's hut which we have nearly completed. The huts are all very indifferently fitted & let in rain and

---

[1] Sir William Howard Russell CVO (1820 – 1907) an Irish reporter with The Times, perhaps the most known of the first war correspondents. He spent 22 months reporting events during the Crimean War, including the Siege of Sebastopol and the Charge of the Light Brigade, leaving Crimea in December 1855. His reports greatly influenced public opinion back in England and reputedly led Florence Nightingale to campaign and then set up improved conditions for the injured and dying soldiers.

wind, do what you will. Every man of the Regt is housed and we have hardly a tent standing. We heard last week of the capitulation of Kars but as yet have heard nothing in print of it, a great pity after the licking the Russians received.

I am sorry to hear Johnnie Coventry has been so ill. I will look him up as soon as he comes out. No drafts have come up lately, we have I hear three captains at Malta; I wish they would come here. Prescott & myself are the only two fit for duty, Ellis being Brevet Major goes on another roster & does not take guard & picquets. Except Ellis, Collings & myself there are no old hands and Mundy does all he can to spoil them. Fancy his putting a fellow in arrest & after the affair was settled, chaffing him about having caught him. Of course this <u>is private</u>. How can one expect youngsters to mind men or respect him when one moment he's chaffing and next reprimanding them. Taking the young ones together they are a good set – but being ignorant of almost everything relating to duty, that style of conducting work is not likely to teach them.

Dick I suppose is in England. Tell him to write again me an account of his proceedings. I heard through Carr's brother in the 39th that another Carr and Dick were going home together from Constantinople which looks as if he had missed the Cunard boat for Smyrna & Egypt. If he sent any of the things I asked him from Constantinople I have never received them. I went on board the 'Bauhaute' on her return and found she had nothing for me. If you have a … will you send me a water barrel with glass ends, the same as the one you gave me last year? My barrel was smashed when I was away at Malta at the time Prescott got so badly hit, he had it with him. Prescott is all right again but greatly disfigured, he was a very good looking fellow but now he is minus the whole of his upper front teeth which were very perfect & has a great scar all along his nose & a bit out of his left nostril, is it not a pity?

Gaspard Tupper I have not seen for an age, nor Milly, they are so far off. Tom Pakenham is all right, I have seen him within the last 10 days.

The Docks, I am told are quite ready to be blown up, indeed someone read the work of destruction was to commence today but as I have not heard any loud explosions conclude it is not the case.

Pretyman, Ellis, Trent & I dine together on Tuesday, we intend to have a capital dinner, turtle soup, fish, game, saddle of mutton & champagne, mulled port and I shall not forget to drink all your good healths.

The French have I hear 25 men away through sickness, I do not mean they die but go into hospital. Our men are very healthy, well supplied with winter clothing of all kinds & rations good. The French have had all extra allowances stopped since the taking of Sebastopol. We have not more that 10 or 12 men in hospital (Regt.) there & light cases.

I really must bring this to a close, goodbye, love to all & believe me always dear John, your affectionate brother

Basil.

Written by Thomas Basil Fanshawe - to his brother-in-law, Edward Denison - copied by TBF's mother.
Camp before Sebastopol
Xmas Eve (1855)

My dear Den

"Better late than never"& my conduct not exactly right, as the saying goes, I will try and be a better correspondent for the future. Our present camp life is monotonous in the extreme but anything is preferable to the trench work. Since the road making ceased, there is scarcely anything to do but look for the arrival of the mail, which now are generally late. The mail of the 30th of November came in after that of the 3 & 7 December.

In one of the papers there is a talk of peace, if matters are squared I do not think there will be a soul sober in camp when the news is known. When men say they have not had enough of fighting I cannot believe them. By the way Pretyman was dining with Sir W Codrington last night and heard that the 33rd & 88th were to go to Gibraltar in the Spring to reorganize preparing to go to relieving the 52 & 43 who are now in India. I can hardly make up my mind how it would suit me. To be boiled for 15 years in that climate is not a very pleasant look out, but it may be only a report.

I have just returned from Balaclava where I have been to see Bayliff who arrived in the Crimea on Saturday from Malta. He is on guard over a lot of land transport men who became unruly at Malta, consequently the authorities packed off Bayliff at 2 hours notice with 30 of our men to have an eye over the L.T. Corps. He cannot leave the ship till this corps disembark. I do not think him looking so well or so stout as when we were at the Vicarage together last year but it may be fancy on my part, perhaps the society and hills in that hothouse Malta may have also something to do with it. I hope he will stand this climate, he will not have to go into a tent as there is room for him in the officer's hut, but he will have to be doubled up with someone – practically everyone has a stove in the compartment he owns and the place is not very cold.

We have had some regular stingers on Tuesday and Wednesday last, the thermometers being 6 degrees above zero – it has however moderated but we have had a frost nearly every night. I have only 1 blanket, 1 great coat and I drape them on my bed & with the exception of one night found it warm enough. We get capital wood from the 'blood stained mess' but it burns out too fast in a stove, charcoal is better.

Since the cold weather set in, lots of swans, geese and wild fowl and bustards[1] have been seen & shot - the bustards have chiefly fallen to the Highland Division in Marmara - they are magnificent fellows I hear & weigh about 21 or 22 pounds. The ducks frequent to Tchenaya but as the Russians pop at you if you pop at the ducks, the game becomes hardly worth the trouble. You have no idea of the filth the roads get into (I do not mean the road the men worked at) that is in first rate order. I came up that way today but went down by the Telegraph, which Dick knows, at the top of the Woronzoff road. I very near broke my neck as my horse was not coupled, our blacksmith was in the guard room drunk, & of course, all neighbouring forges had plenty of customers.

---

[1] The Bustard's habitat is grassland or steppe - flat or rolling landscapes and is also found on undisturbed cultivation, preferring areas with wild or cultivated crops such as cereals, vineyards and fodder plants. Breeding in southern and central Europe, and across temperate Asia, the European populations are mainly resident, but Asian birds move further south in winter. No doubt TBF would have been delighted to report sight of this bird as the bustard had been hunted out of existence in Britain by the 1840s. A programme of re-introduction was started between Russia and Britain in this new millennium.

The French blew up their part of the Docks on Tuesday last. Our side, I hear is not to be ready for some time as the water has got into the shafts & must be pumped out.

Milly Tupper I saw yesterday, he had walked over to the 50th camp. He had just returned from taking the powder (about 8 tons) into Sebastopol which is to blow up our port. He said the clever authorities kept the waggons and horses for a full half hour quite in sight of the Russians, who luckily did not fire either a shot or a shell at the party. Completely to destroy the Docks or rather to prevent the Russians from fitting them up again with the same material, the granite blocks of which the docks are built, are to be smashed to atoms – otherwise it would be easy to replace the blocks. This is I believe, much easier said than done.

On my way home I met Gaspard Tupper, I also saw him last week, he is looking very fresh. Did I tell you the 4th Division has got up theatricals performer officers - I understand they are first rate? I was to have gone to see them tonight but was put off by the men who invited me to a future day. Wednesday last I dined in Ladies Society, the first time I have spoken to one since I left Malta. I dined with our Brigadier & his wife, General[1] & Mrs Straubenzee[2] – a very pleasant evening, she is a jolly nice little woman – I cannot but think it must be a very stupid life for her, she never sees a lady for the very simple reason, there are none. Every Saturday night in the 4th Division a regular cyder cellar is held - General Trollope[3] at one end of the table and General Jarrett Vice – I am told there are some

---

[1] General Sir Charles Thomas van Straubenzee GCB (1812 – 1892), Commander of 1st Brigade of the Light Division took both assaults on the Redan during the Siege of Sevastopol, 1862 appointed Commander of British Troops in China and Hong Kong and Governor of Malta.

[2] Mrs van Straubenzee - Charlotte Louisa Richardson, daughter of General John Luther Richardson.

[3] General Sir Charles Trollope K.C.B. (1808 – 1888) - 53rd Regiment of Foot (second cousin of the novelist Anthony Trollope).

capital songs sang & am thinking of going next week. Did I tell you the Land Transport Corps is gone to grief, we have now to tend our own horses for forage. Fancy their leaving in one week – 1,170 horses and mules, pretty well out of 14,000 which is the total strength.

I have not a word more of camp intelligence except that we are still bothered by fleas. I thought the cold weather would have killed them.

I wrote to John last Monday and suppose the letter would reach him while at the Vicarage – will you tell him and my mother their letters of the 30th November and 3 & 7 December have reached me. Many thanks dear Den for the cheese and toaster you and Helen have kindly sent me, it will be most useful and acceptable. How I wish I could be with you all tomorrow to wish you in person a merry Xmas and happy new year, let us hope we may have the next together. The [access] major has knocked a second time for my letter so must conclude with much love to all both at Parsloes & the Vicarage. Tell my Mother I have just received the red flannel from young Brook of the Regt. the direction had been washed off and I only knew of its arrival from Milly. My hands are so cold I can scarcely write.

Goodbye & believe me always

Your most affectionate

Basil Fanshawe

Written by Thomas Basil Fanshawe – to his father, Revd. Thomas Lewis Fanshawe.
Camp Sebastopol
December 28th 1855

My Dearest Governor

I hope you will not be surprised by not having received an answer to your last but the mail only arrived last Saturday, some accident having delayed the vessel. I have written to John and Edward the last two mails & am afraid this will be anything but a lively document, nothing of importance or anything out of common routine of camp life having taken place since Monday. First let me thank you and the Missus very much for your letters and also for the box you have despatched, & I have no doubt it will eventually turn up.

Xmas day we passed much as any Sunday out here. In the evening Pretyman, Ellis, Trent and I dined together and had a first rate dinner with stacks of drink. On the whole, I passed the evening pleasantly enough, considering I was in Crimea and not at the Vicarage at Dagenham. How I longed to be with you. I hope you all had a merry Xmas & look forward to a Happy New Year. I hear the whole of us are going to dine together on that day and I believe a lot of drink is going to be given on promotion.

Bayliff arrived in Crimea yesterday and dined with me last night. I certainly think he is not looking so broad or so stout as last year, but otherwise looking well. Three other young gents came up today – Crosse, Elliott and Browne[1]. I have not seen them yet. It seems very strange that we cannot get a Captain up - we have only Prescott and myself to do Regt work & all the fault of the officer commanding!

---

[1] Lt. H. Crosse & Lt. G. Elliott & Lt. A. Browne – 33rd Regiment - arrived in Crimea 29th December 1855.

Our weather has been unsettled the last two or three days. Yesterday we had a fog as thick as a genuine London one and mostly greasy under foot. It froze hard last night and today it has been a freezer. I did not venture further than the Victoria Redoubt (as you have Dick now at your elbow he will give you a much clearer account of the different places than I can by pen) just to show Bayliff the town & works of the place. He seems very blood thirsty & wishes that he could have an idea of how the siege was conducted. I think after 48 hours trenches his curiosity would have been fully satisfied, mine was!

I am writing this under difficulties for the table is rickety & stands on the floor of our new mess hut which (the floor) gives pleasantly to every footstep that passes in the room, rather resembling a springboard. We have built a brick fireplace in one of the doorways and made it pretty comfortable. Last night in honour of Bayliff's arrival we had some singing and B favoured us with several. Today the mail brought me a letter from my Mother of the 15th and one from Helen. Thanks for the recipes for the soup and mash which I shall put in practice at once. I hope you enjoyed your trip to the cattle show[1] and theatre[2]. I have not been able to get to the 4th Division theatre although offered a ticket last night. I have been

---

[1] Prince Albert opened the new Metropolitan Cattle Market in June 1855 (later Caledonian Market) and by removing the live cattle from the old Smithfield site, the new market could 'show' up to 7000 head of cattle and 26000 sheep. A newspaper report of the market show of 22 December tells how the public attended in their thousands and among the exhibitors of prize cattle was the Prince Consort.

[2] TBF may have been referring to a theatre visit that took place on 26th December - Boxing Day and traditional for pantomimes. In 1855 the Theatre Royal Covent Garden offered 'Ye belle alliance', Sadlers Wells performed 'Harlequin Puss in Boots', The Queen's 'St. George and the Dragon', Victoria 'Harlequin and the five senses' and the Theatre Royal, Drury Lane 'Hey Diddle Diddle'. We cannot know which if any of those were chosen but we can confirm from the descriptions preserved in the Lord Chamberlains Licence records that most of those plays contained topical references, including comments concerning Crimea.

rather bothered with cold and cough but nothing to signify and so thought it more prudent to stay at home.

The latest shave today is that Omar Pasha[1] with his army has been taken prisoner – rather a sell this. I hear the French do not see the pull of going into Asia and in fact <u>won't</u>. I hear the rumour of which I told Edward, about our going to India has been unfounded and now the 7th & 23rd Regt are to accompany us. <u>It's all bosh</u> and also most contradictory about peace. How pleasant if they could ignore it. Tell Mother that little Ellis who she asked about is now about 6 feet high and coming out to Kertch having got some staff appointment there. Lacy, I do not fancy we shall ever see out here and he is now too well up the list to retire or go into another Regt if peace comes off. He is a big fence for me to get over. I think the rest above me will not be too much in my way.

Thank my Mother for sending me the Daily News[2] but we <u>now</u> take it in with lots of other papers but if she will continue sending some of the latest Times it will suit me better as I can give them to the men & Sergeants.

I heard from Malta - Bayliff bringing me up a parcel in which I found a note from Eleanor, very gay they appear to be there. Tell Helen that the polka that she made is most comfortable and warm and just the thing for wearing under a shell jacket[3]. I got one of the fur coats which Dick wanted so much to get, but after having it a

---

[1] Omar Pasha (real name Omar or Mihajlo Latas) 1806–1871. An Ottoman general and governor who was born in the territory of the Austrian Empire to Serbian Orthodox Christian parents. When faced with charges of embezzlement, he fled to Bosnia under Ottoman rule and converted to Islam. Joining the Ottoman Army he was quickly promoted and took responsibility of quashing several rebellions. As a commander in the Crimean War he participated in the Siege of Sevastopol.

[2] The Daily News was founded & edited by Charles Dickens in 1846 (editor in 1855 - William Weir).

[3] Short woollen jacket, with a high stiff collar and a cropped in waist.

few days they sent an order to recall them, much to my disgust, but I have lots of clothes and have now got a long pair of boots which are pretty good.

I walked over to Milly yesterday, he is suffering from a slight cold but otherwise all right. I have seen Gaspard twice the last week – fresh as possible. Billy has failed in his endeavour for a substantive rank but with his service he could hardly expect to get it. I have had pretty fair luck this year & hope it will not desert me next in the way of promotion. Tell John I got his last with copy certificate, I must stop with best love to all at the Vicarage and Parsloes and earnestly wish I could be with you.

Goodbye, dearest Gov & believe me ever your most affectionate son

Basil

I know this must be stupid but I would rather it should be, than not to let another mail pass without writing.

Written by Thomas Basil Fanshawe - to his mother.
Camp Sebastopol
January 17th (1856)

My Dearest Mother

I fully intended writing on Monday the last mail day but was prevented by having to struggle down to Balaclava on a board and did not return till 6 o'clock. There is no news so I shall tell you the small amount I can from what I have put down in my diary. I wrote to Dick on the 7th. My cold has nearly gone and does not bother me at all. I have got into a new hut with a place all to myself, much better & larger than the old long officers hut, it is much more waterproof, in fact quite so and I am quite satisfied with the change. There are two youngsters on the other side who are very quiet.

The last mail brought me your letter of 24th December & one from Edward, many thanks – and a whole heap of papers which I gave Mrs Straubenzee to look at. Did I tell you I had dined there? She is a very jolly little woman but must I imagine, find this sort of life slow in the extreme, especially as she cannot ride out, having no side saddle.

On Friday last I went with the 48th and went to the 4th Division theatricals which were first rate. I tried hard to get a bill to enclose, but failed. The pieces performed were a phenomena in a smock frock & the moustache movement. I was in shouts the whole time. 'Lord A Russell's Rifle Brigade' was capital. Lacy[1] of the 63rd looked & acted as a woman uncommonly well. After the performance I adjourned to the 68th mess where singing commenced and was kept up till about 2. I got home about ½ two, being pitch dark & the ground greasy and beastly, it was no joke steeple chasing over the

---

[1] Lt. G. Lacy - 63rd Regiment – arrived Crimea 3rd September 1855.

drains which abound in every camp. I slipped twice into a drain without damage.

Saturday I dined with the 48th again with Picket's brother who gave a dinner on his promotion - stacks of drink & dinner good. It came on a thick fog & when I left about two ½, I could not see a yard before me. I had a lantern & tried to find my way but found myself in the lines of the 57th Regt not knowing where I had got to, so gave up the idea of finding my way & as I was riding my old pony, which Dick rode when out here, I trusted to his good bringing me home, which he did about three.

It came on to rain on Sunday which lasted all day. About six o'clock it froze a regular stinger and it certainly was the coldest night I have felt out here. Snowing at the same time. On Monday it was bitterly cold and I had to go to Balaclava on a board which lasted all day. I walked there and back & I got down all right but coming home up the hill with the snow and rain in ones face was a bother and no mistake. Tuesday took sick, I dined with Chatfield[1] 49th at their mess, many inquiries after him. They have a very good mess and very comfortable, had John singing and supper, home ¼ to four yesterday.

I rode to Balaclava (Tuesday it thawed), to see if the "Harbinger"[2] came in and any chance of getting the box you sent me. She is a Kasatch & expected to arrive daily. I hope she will. I got last mail

---

[1] Lt. George Kemp Chatfield (1834-1862) - 49th Regiment of Foot.

[2] On 14 November 1854 the *Harbinger* was in Balaclava Harbour when a gale struck. She suffered extensive damage, losing the figurehead, cat heads, forecastle rails, poop rails, side ladders and much of the outside work was broken. However the hull, machinery and masts were in good condition and she was able to help in the rescue of the crew of the *Prince* which lay severely damaged outside the harbour. *Harbinger* was fit to sail from Scutari on 12 January 1855 and arrived at Malta 6 days later. The ship carrying wounded men from the battles of Alma, Inkermann and Balaclava eventually arrived at Portsmouth on 6th February.

Messrs Hayter & Howell's[1] notice that they had sent a box per Harbinger No 6614 as she must have a tidy lot & I trust mine will be one of the first landed.

I called on Gaspard on my way home but he was not in - I hear he is alright again. Two days back an officer of the 46th – Messenger[2] by name, an acting engineer got killed through his own carelessness. He was engaged in blasting and the fuse to the mine being a long while going off, he foolishly went up to ascertain the reason. Just as he got to the spot, it went off & blew his head clean off. I did not know him.

Today I am on picquet consequently confined to Camp. I am going to dine with Bunbury of the 23rd tonight, my old Captain. I hear they have a very good mess but I shall be able to tell you more about it tomorrow.

The Russians are pretty quiet in the way of firing. The remainder of the forts were blown up last Tuesday. I think I have said my little all. Peter and Trent who mess with me, went down to Scutari on Monday for a fortnight, for their own amusement, I suppose it will be the end of the month before they are back. The mail is just signalised so I suppose I shall hear how you passed Xmas. Everyone, tell Dick, sends their best thanks for taking charge & delivering the different parcels committed to his charge. Pray thank Aunt Mourant[3] for her two pounds. I do not think I could fill a letter to her from here, especially as she must have had descriptions enough from Master Billy who I hear is a better reporter and thinks

---

[1] A successful family business of military packers and merchants based in South-East London. The owner, Sir Thomas Howell was also Director of Contracts to the War Office from 1855 to 1874.

[2] Lt. John Horndon Messenger – 46th Regiment - killed by a mine on a road on 15th January 1856.

[3] Great Aunt to TBF – Sophia Mourant, sister of maternal grandmother, Mary Le Marchant, nee Carey.

himself hardly used in not getting more leave. Gaspard, I hear thinks he ought to have him made a C.B.

How glad you must have been when the sale was over. I only wish I could have had the chance of helping you. I wrote to Edward about three mails back. The receipts you sent me are very useful. I am living, during Trent's absence, with Ellis and his servant is cook and is a first rate hand – mine is having a holiday.
Have you heard of a tenant for Parsloes yet – when do Helen and Edward go? I did not find out yesterday if the Bacchaute was in but I will ask about the flash which Dick found from me. The Steward said nothing about it to me when I went on board to see if he had brought me anything in the shape of vegetables or poultry, which he had not.

Friday 18th, I had a very jolly dinner last night with Bunbury who asked particularly after the Governor. On my return to camp I found your letter of the 31st, the only one I got and some papers. Today, another mail just arrived brought me a lot of papers and a letter from John of the 4th and I am glad to find all so flourishing, how I should like to have been with you at Xmas.

I hear there is no chance of peace! I hope to hear next mail that the tenant you mention as possible to become an inmate of Parsloes has decided on taking the place. I have been engaged all morning on that intellectual pursuit – road making. It turned to snow last night, we had about 3 inches this morning on the ground. I had to be up at 4½ for picquet & it was snowing then. By the way, the use of an inlying picquet is to lie away to turn out at a moment's notice in case of a [xxx] or fire, but I believe we are the only brigade in the British Army to turn out at reveille.

It has been a lovely day today, cold with bright sun, but tonight it is going to freeze sharp. Fancy Johnny Le Marchant writing to me this mail from Paris. He seems in great spirits and becoming a regular Eton boy in his expressions. His leg he tells me, the doctor he saw, will be all right. I have not heard from Malta since Bayliff came up. I fancy Eleanor is too busy with all the gaiety going on, to find much time for writing.

Best love to the Governor, Dick and all at Parsloes – and the same to yourself, Believe me, ever dearest Mother, your most affectionate son

Basil

Written by Thomas Basil Fanshawe - to his brother, John Gaspard Fanshawe - copied by his mother.
Camp before Sebastopol
January 25th (1856)

My dearest John

Many thanks for your last two letters, the one of the 11 arrived yesterday & I also heard from my Mother. I am afraid of letting the post go without a line but I really have hardly anything worth telling, the sight of my hand writing is I suppose something.

Our weather has been mild in the extreme since this day week when I wrote to my Mother, & we are wading up to our ankles in the Crimean mud. We have had some drenching rain but my new hut has not let in a drop and I am very comfortable and cosy in it. The Russians fire now & then on the town with very little damage, I have not been down for some time but it is coming very near my turn for duty there. I hope I shall not be on guard in the Redan again.

This is a lovely day but I am on regular picquet with my company and so cannot go out of camp besides which, I have been President of a Regiment Court Martial and tried two prisoners. I had to write the proceedings myself so you see we have something to do! Our Brigadier has also taken it into his head to have the Brigade out 2 or 3 times a week. Saturday and Monday & today the Brigade has been at drill – we seldom get back before 1 o'clock.

On Tuesday everyone was full of peace which was communicated by Admiral Freemantle[1] at Constantinople to Sir W Codrington. I need not say how anxious we all are to know if it's the case – fancy, we meeting again! Almost too good to be true! The only people who I imagine would regret the change are the D.A.2.M gents and D.A.A. gents who of course would not like to resign their good berths. There is a diversity of opinion which will be the plan of the next campaign, no one really knows anything and the shaves are numerous – either Asia or the Principalities seem most in favour out here.

The Theatre is in full force but I have not been very lately. There is a first rate billiard table at Donnybrook which is much patronised. We are getting up a glee club in our Brigade. Bayliff of course forms one of its members, there are several fellows with good voices. I passed a most pleasant hour with the 7th two nights ago, we had some capital songs after mess – which is first rate. Tonight, I dine out with Straubenzee our Brigadier. Things are getting very dear and scarce - fancy pork 4 pounds a pound, potatoes 5 pence a lb, almost a penny each. The Harbinger has not come round from [Kasale] Bay and I have seen nothing of my box yet.

Wednesday I went over to see Tom Pakenham who is looking very fresh. After lunch I rode with him to the 50th. He promised to come & see me in a few days, if so I will give him your messages – Did I ever tell you that dining one night with the 68 I met Daniels[2] of the 38th. John D brother, he heard my name mentioned and soon found

---

[1] Charles Freemantle, promoted to Rear Admiral in 1854 he was subsequently appointed Flag Officer at the port of Balaclava in April 1855 after Rear-Admiral Boxer had died of cholera. His main task was to sort out the many problems concerning transportation and bring order to a chaotic supply system. He was relatively successful and when hostilities ceased he oversaw the orderly and safe evacuation of the troops and all the ancillary staff.
[2] Brevet Major C. F. Daniels - 38th Regiment - 3rd Division.

out who I was, he seems a quiet gentlemanly fellow, I did not see much of him that night & have not met since.

The paper hunts are still in favour but the guard is so tremendously heavy it's very hard messing – we expect Barrett and another captain soon. Pretyman and Trent are not yet returned from their trip to Constantinople.

I am glad to learn Bab is so well and you don't mention the chick - I suppose he's flourishing, I shall not know him again.

By all accounts Russell[1], I believe left the Crimea because it suited him and for no other reason. We have now nearly 500 men in the Regiment here & if they sent up a couple of good strong drafts we shall make a decent appearance if we take the full again.

Best love to all, believe me to be your affectionate brother

Basil.

---

[1] Russell left Crimea in December 1855 and was replaced by the Constantinople correspondent of The Times.

Written by Thomas Basil Fanshawe - to his mother.
Camp Sebastopol
February 8th 1856

My dearest Mother

The mail has just arrived bringing me a letter from Helen. On Tuesday last I got a letter from both John and you. Helen said she had been dining the night before she wrote, at the Vicarage and that both the Governor and yourself were suffering but I hope long ere this that both of you are quite recovered. Since I got rid of my cold I have been as well as can be and look forward with some degree of certainty of seeing you all again within 6 months now that everything seems so like peace. How delighted we shall all be to meet again.

We heard out here some days back that an armistice had been signed but Sir Wm Codrington has not yet received the official notification of the fact. It was merely telegraphed by General Storks[1] at Constantinople. The latest shave here is that either the Light or 25th Division are to be removed to Balaclava for the performance of fatigue duties – <u>a very pleasant prospect</u> indeed if after having made oneself comfortable up here, to be encamped there. The only thing they will say is that whichever division is moved, that division will go next after the Guards to England. This I do not believe but I do think that the Light and Second Division will be of the first batch to clear out, especially if as John says we are to proceed to India. If we do, I think I can see my way to either Senior Captain or Junior

---

[1] Lieutenant-General Sir Henry Knight Storks GCB, GCMG (1811 – 1874) soldier and colonial governor. With the rank of Major General, Storks superintended the British bases set up in Ottoman territory during the Crimean War, where he supported the nursing efforts of Florence Nightingale. After the war, he served in the War Office as Secretary for Military Correspondence before taking up diplomatic and colonial appointments.

Major. I have now Pretyman, Fitzgerald, Quayle, Lacy and Wickham, ahead of these Peter I think is certain to go, as India would not suit him, Fitz would not leave. Quayle, I think would. It will be a great shame and very hard lines if Lacy is allowed to return to the regiment, his appointment ought to be made a permanent one. Wickham, I hear is to go before a medical board in March to see if he is able to serve or go on half pay as captain with a pension of £100 a year. Col. Johnstone would like to go but I hear it would not agree with him. Murray is certain to remain unless married, as John has heard unmarried. Collings would go out, Donovan I doubt ever joining but may exchange. I think I have a fair prospect of moving and there it is quite possible to effect an exchange. I would much sooner not go out but if we are ordered, of course it would be very foolish to exchange. Some think if we must come back to England to recruit & at least 18 months or more must elapse before we can be ready. At present I am the first captain with the regiment (I do not mean those on the regiment staff) for leave and if I could get it, supposing an armistice is signed, I think it would be far more agreeable to return to England than remain here. What should I gain from remaining out?

I suppose Helen by this time has received my last of this day week. The weather then was most beastly snow and then snow & thaw. Snow heavy again on Saturday, then on Sunday. Since lovely weather in the day, like Spring but sharp frosts at night, particularly Tuesday night when everything in my room was frozen. On Wednesday I was on guard in the Woronzoff road with Bayliff who exchanged duties to come down with me, much to my delight, as otherwise I should have had to pass 26 hours with a (towering) snob of an Irishman as my companion. Benwell[1] by name, Dick I think knows the bloke. We had a double tent but as we could not have a fire inside we found it pretty chilly at night. The Russians have been firing very heavily this week - cause unknown, except the warm

---

[1] Lt. F. Benwell - 33rd Regiment - arrived in Crimea 26th September 1855.

weather tempted them to fire. About 1½ o'clock on Monday last the French blew up Fort Nicholas[1]. I saw it from just by the 34th camp. Dick knows the spot. We were inspected on that day by our general, Lord Wm Paulet[2] so I could not go down close. It was a very pretty sight to see the Fort go up, or rather the thick smoke, as after the first mine was exploded the smoke prevented you seeing much. There were five or more mines which went off, one after the other and most effectually cleared the place out pretty quick as a (Yankee) would have it. The Ruskies appeared astonished but contrary to their usual custom did not begin firing.

I think that is about all that has happened since my last. The road continues in a beastly state - not the road to Balaclava made by the men that is in very good order considering the numerous amount of traffic. Yesterday, on returning from guard, I opened your long expected box which I had sent down to Balaclava for, the day previous. Many thanks for the contents which were in capital presentation except the apples which were nearly all rotten. I got about nine fit for use, and a bottle of ginger broke but I speedily transferred the contents to another bottle. Tell Den and Helen with my best love and thanks, that the cheese toaster and cheese was tried & highly approved of by all tasting, last night. The shirts will be most useful on guard, ditto the gloves.

I am very sorry to find by Helen's letter that Col. & Mrs Sullivan have doubts about taking the house but she (Helen) says there are

---

[1] Positioned on the most northern point at the entrance into the dockyard harbour.
[2] Field Marshal Lord William Paulet, GCB (1804 – 1893) served as Assistant Adjutant-General of the Cavalry Division, under Lord Lucan, at the Battle of Alma in September 1854, at the Battle of Balaklava in October 1854 and at the Battle of Inkerman in November 1854 as well as at the Siege of Sevastopol after which he was given command of the rear area, including the Bosphorus, Gallipoli and the Dardanelles before returning to England. By 1865 he had been appointed Adjutant-General to the Forces.

more applicants. How glad I shall be to hear of your getting a desirable tenant.

She also informs me of Charles Gostling having had a paralytic stroke, what an affliction. By the way, the family seem to have been unfortunate lately, what with Helen Le Marchant's[1] broken leg and Aunt Tupper's[2] accident. I hope they are all going on well.

I went this day week to the Rifle Theatre in our brigade, the acting was very good but it was not quite up to the 4th Division, but then the latter have the whole division to choose from. The 7th, ourselves and the 23rd, which comprise our brigade (bar 54th) are all talking about getting theatricals but this move to Balaclava, should it come, will sadly knock on the head all these arrangements.

Ellis left us today on his way home. I am very sorry he has gone – a capital good fellow when you know him. I hear from the 49th and the 39th fellows of Fan and Billy who say it is an awful place but I would not mind exchanging places with either.

I hope Dick is all right again. Best love to the Gov and love to all at Parsloes, the same to yourself and believe me ever dearest Mother, your most affectionate son

Basil

---

[1] 1st Cousin - 19 year old eldest daughter of Sir Denis Le Marchant, brother of TBF's mother.
[2] Mother's sister, Anna Maria Tupper.

I have not heard from Malta for an age. Eleanor seems to have forgotten I am still in existence. I shall write to Helen on Monday and after condoling about Charles, request Eleanor to send up some dresses etc. for theatricals - she sent up a box for the Rifles. I am going to try the plum pudding tonight and let you know the result in my next - I am sure it must be good. I have already caught a mouse in the trap.

Written by Thomas Basil Fanshawe - to his brother, John Gaspard Fanshawe.
Camp Sebastopol
February 15th (1856)

My dearest John

Yesterday, wonderful to say the mail came in on the day that it was due and brought me your last of the 2nd I presume, but it was not dated and the day before the other mail, yours of the 28th. There is hardly anything fresh, our expected chief Mundy is laid up from a kick from a mule and goes hobbling about with the 2 sticks, making as his leg much worse than it really is. We hear that Johnstone is coming out, this will send M home, provided the authorities give him leave. He is sure to apply for leave and most likely get it as he has been out the whole time. I wish they would both go. Peter I am certain from what he told me yesterday will take substantive and go into some other regiment. If I only could be sure Lacy could not be brought back to the regiment, I should not despair of being junior major before the next 18 months. Pity I believe is not for purchase. Quayle and Wickham, I am certain could never go to India nor would Donovan, I think.

Our weather has been pretty fine the past week, on Monday they marched the regiment down to Balaclava to change the muskets, giving us Enfield[1] ones in place of the Minié[2], a great improvement but of course they mismanaged the thing and (large) without any clasp to relieve it.

---

[1] The Enfield Pattern 1853 rifle-musket (also known as Pattern 1853 Enfield, P53 Enfield or Enfield rifle-musket) was a .577 calibre Minié-type muzzle-loading rifle-musket, used by the British Army from 1853 to 1867.
[2] French invented Pattern 1851 Minié rifle was in use by the British Army from 1851 to 1855.

Did I tell you Col. Sullivan[1], who came to look at Parsloes was A. A. General or something of the kind to our division when we left home & went away from bad health. I hope you have by this heard that Parsloes is again occupied or rather is to be, on best going & a nice tenant. Surely it would suit some of the applicants.

Poor Dick, I am sorry to hear is again seedy, how unlucky he is. Many enquiries after him here from fellows he knew. The 'Bauhaute', tell him is gone from here, but if I can find his flask I will do the handsome and store it. Connell has not yet sent Tillbrook's[2] pipe up & he is living, I believe at Kannara with the Highlanders, a devil of a way off. I am delighted to find the Gov all right & Bab and the chick so flourishing - the last I shall not know when I see him which I certainly hope shall be within in the next 6 months.

The work of demolition in the town of Sebastopol goes on – the French blew up Fort Alexander[3] the day we went to Balaclava so I did not see it. The aqueduct[4] was blown up the day before yesterday and part of the white building (Barracks) the day before – we are now pulling the Redan into bits and getting the guns out of it. The Regt siege train left us today, all the bands of this brigade at their head playing 'Should Old Acquaintance be forgot' for Balaclava, there to embark for England – lucky dogs!

I have had to share my division of the hut with young Thistlethwayte[5], brother of the one[6] who died of cholera in the Regt,

---

[1] Colonel William Sullivan C.B., Assistant Adjutant General – Staff appointment.

[2] Capt. P. Tillbrook - 50th Regiment – arrived in Crimea 22nd August 1855.

[3] On the headland directly north of Sebastopol.

[4] In the Russian army sector, between the Inkerman Ridge and the Valley of the River Tchernaya.

[5] Lt. Augustus Frederick Thistlethwayte - 33rd Regiment – arrived in Crimea, 13th February 1856.

[6] Lt. Arthur Henry Thistlethwayte - Scots Fusiliers 1st Battalion – arrived in Crimea 14th September 1854, transferred to 2nd Battalion and died November 1854.

in Sept '54. He is a nice quiet boy and from what I have seen of him, he only came up on Wednesday, like him. I have come to the end of my paper which I much doubted being able to fill, as it is I am afraid it is a stupid affair but nothing is going on. The roads have dried up wonderfully. Today there is a great paper turnout at Head Quarters.

Mr Kettle[1] came & paid me a visit on Sunday. He says they have not much to do & expect to return soon. I gave him a county paper which pleased him. He appears to thrive on Crimean air & diet.

Best love to all at home and the same Bab, the chick and yourself. Believe me ever dearest John, your most affectionate brother

Basil

I have been writing this with a vile [perishing] steel pen – Bayliff is all serene & desires to be remembered. I saw Johnson today. The Ruskies have been firing more than usual this morning or their mining operations have been going on extensively.

Goodbye

I have not seen the Tuppers for an age!

---

[1] Probably Private James Kettle - 47th Foot (Lancashire Regiment) - wounded at the Battle of Alma on 20 September 1854. The Kettle family (sometime Kittle) had been resident in the village of Dagenham for many years. During the 1850s George Kittle was the landlord of the Bull Inn near the centre of the village, a short walk from the Vicarage occupied by TBF's family. The Bull Inn was also the local post office, where the post chase collected and delivered the post from the inhabitants of Dagenham. A son of George Kittle is listed as the local post runner in the local directories of this period.

British Army Post Office. Constantinople (1855)

Illustrated London News 19th January 1856

Eduard Ivanovich Totleben

Vezenberg & Co., St. Petersburg (1880 - 1886)

Library of Congress

'William Howard Russell, esqr., the Times Special Correspondent'

Roger Fenton (1855)

Library of Congress

'The Artist's van'

Roger Fenton (1855) - Library of Congress

'A Zouave' - Roger Fenton dressed in a
borrowed uniform, sitting on a chair

Marcus Sparling (1855) - Library of Congress

Written by Thomas Basil Fanshawe - to his mother.
Camp Sebastopol
February 22nd 1856

[Written at top of page]
The weather has been very cold at night but fine during the day, it looks like rain tonight.
I believe I get off seeing the man being hung tomorrow.

My dearest Mother

I got your last of the 6th on Wednesday and thanks for it. I wrote to John last week which I suppose you have seen, since which nothing out of the common has happened. Carr returned from leave last Wednesday, looking very fresh – it is a great pull for us as captains to get him again, no one even thought it likely if he would again. I hear another Wallis[1] is on his way from Malta, this will be a good thing.

I have had a very busy week this week, not a day to myself. Monday I went on guard in the Woronzoff road & about as cold a day as I ever had the pleasure of being out in, even in America. I took the guard for one officer of the 7th whose turn it was but as he was a principal character in their theatre, which came off that night and a whole heap of swells coming, they would have been obliged to put off the performance would they not have got someone to take it. In consequence of my having done it, the 7th have made (me) an honorary member of their theatre. So I think I have got the best of it, especially as I was first for guard & this guard is one of the best we find – and I also got off inlying picquet in the field and Captain of the day, which would have entailed on me two court martials.

---

[1] Lt. A. Wallis - 33rd Regiment – arrived in Crimea 14 September 1854, wounded 21 November 1854.

I took down heaps of things & though we had only a double hut, I did not find it very cold. Sir Wm. Codrington was to have reviewed the whole of the six divisions of infantry on the heights in rear of the Redoubt's Camp, but the weather was so bad it was put off. I suppose there would have been some thirty thousand men out. It would have been a fine sight & I am rather glad it did not come off as I should have missed seeing it. I hear that Sir W is going to see us on Monday if the weather is fine. The divisions have all been practicing this week, preparing for it. Our Brigade was out both Thursday and today. I escaped today as yesterday being on a working party I got a blister on my heel and was not at all sorry of an excuse today. Tomorrow morning I hear that we parade at an early hour for the purpose of hanging that ruffian in the 77th who while acting as orderly in their hospital, smashed an unfortunate artilleryman's head in, who was a patient, with a crow bar. He actually deserves being strung up, although it is not an exhibition I care for. He was to have been despatched some time back but they could not find a man to perform the office of executioner. At last a Land Transport man has been found. He is to receive £5, his discharge and a free passage home.

On Friday last I went to the 48th to dine and 4th Division theatricals after. First rate performance, I send you the bill of the play, also one of the 7th who had a dress rehearsal on Saturday last, to which I went. Young Radcliffe[1] 23rd and Kerr[2] 7th got up very well. The first is too tall but looks well. The other is capital. I do not fancy ours will come off. I was to have written to Eleanor on Monday for the dresses but being on guard could not. I heard from her the same post as yours, she talks of being able to come up and see the Crimea this Spring.

---

[1] Lt. H. Radcliffe - 23rd Regiment – arrived Crimea 23rd February 1855.
[2] Lt. H. Kerr - 7th Regiment – arrived Crimea 6th December 1855.

The place is much altered since the 8th September and the town itself is under a heap of ruins and hard to get wood at all handy. We are now pulling the Redan to bits & the removing [of] guns is steadily going on, there are still a thousand left to bring up. First of these are French which we have undertaken to bring up as their artillery horses are pretty nearly busted up.

I have been interrupted for the last hour & half by fellows coming in but Eleanor said she hopes to see one on board Mr Claris ship. Aunt Mary talks of going to England to meet Charles and his wife on arrival. What an affliction it must be to him.

Tonight I am going to dine with a man of the 97th who I knew of old in Halifax. Gaspard and Milly came up the day before yesterday, both looking fresh and well. I met a man of the 21st the night before last who I have not seen for 10 years, Bennett[1] by name. I stayed at his house once during the short holiday at Shrewsbury[2]. He declared he would not have recognized me, not to be wondered at!

I hope your cold & headache has long vanished without any bad effects. Dick, I trust to hear in your next is rapidly gaining ground. John who wrote to me yesterday says he is wonderfully pulled down. By the way, I have not received an Illustrated since Xmas. I do not care for myself but the men like to see it. The other papers arrive all right.

Richard Bayliff is all right but I do not think he would stand hard work. The kitten that Dick asks about, which Mundy was to have given me, died before it came into my hands, however our mice

---

[1] Lt. John Bennett - 21st Regiment (Fusiliers) at the Siege & Fall of Sebastopol, retired 1867 with rank of Major. Attended Shrewsbury School 1845 -1850.
[2] Shrewsbury School attended by TBF and his younger brother Richard (Dick). The school's reputation for classical education was confirmed by the Public Schools Act 1861 listing it as one of the nine 'great' public schools in England.

traps have cleared all the mice out and they (the traps) are in great request. This mail has set all talking about the strife in America[1] which no one here thinks likely to come off to blows & peace seems more certain than ever. I hope it will come off. I hear that the Horse Guards have the arrangement of how the Divisions are to return home. I hope they will send ours one of the first. A man riding in Sebastopol two days ago had his animal's head carried off by a round shot, close work if true, for the gent on the top. I must shut up as I have not a word more to say & how I got as far as this I do not know. Excuse a stupid letter, with the best love to the Governor, Dick and all at Parsloes.

Believe me ever dearest mother, your most affectionate son

Basil

Peter desires to be remembered - also Bayliff. The Rifles give a swell night at their theatre & supper on Wednesday next to Sir William Codrington. I hope to get a ticket, it is only for those who have served under Sir William as Brigadier of the Light Division.

---

[1] Nominations for the presidential elections in America began in February 1856 with serious conflicting issues among the states regarding slavery, immigration and religious tolerance.

Written by Thomas Basil Fanshawe - to his mother.
Camp Sebastopol
Friday March 14th (1856)

My dearest Mother,

I have had really so little to say what has been going on here that I was ashamed to write the last week and even now there is hardly anything doing. My last was on the 29th to Dick who was by John's letter yesterday, getting round. We have had most changeable weather, snow and rain and some beautiful warm days.

Sunday week was a lovely day and I rode over to the monastery. Yesterday, was another fine day and Collings and I rode all over Sebastopol in perfect safety as the armistice is in operation and of course the Ruskies do not fire unless you ruin the place. You could not believe the heap of ruins, the town is reduced to, nothing but the walls of two or three houses in the French part used by them for their men. A band of theirs yesterday, was playing on what was the Russian promenade of the town, in sight of the Russians, much to their disgust, I should think.

Then we went to look at the docks which are a sight. I picked up a couple of bits of granite to make paper weights for you & also a stunning bit of white marble which belonged to a pillar of one of the churches & which I had to smash with a bar of iron, with some difficulty. I would have brought the whole of it but being on my pony could not fix it. There is hardly anything else to get out of the place except shot of every size of which there are heaps. I mean to bring home one of each of the smaller sort, but as you have seen Dick's they will be without interest to you.

There has been no end of fraternizing between the Russians and allies on the Tchernaya below Inkerman since the armistice came out. Heaps of French go over to the Inkerman ruins & chapel but Codrington is very particular & will not allow the English to pass the line of the aqueduct. Heaps of fellows disregarded this order & were caught by Wickham and Codrington who were furious & told the fellows to make the best of their way back to camp.

I was out shooting about a week ago but only got two shots, one a snap shot at a cock a mile off & the other I slated a wigeon[1] which I ate last night & capital it was. There are such a lot of fellows shooting that (it) is not worthwhile going out.

Everyone here is talking of how soon & by what ships they are to proceed to England. The shave yesterday was that the Baltic Fleet is coming to take the army home & that the Guards and the Light Division are the first to (hope). We ('the Duke's') are undecided if we go in the 'Nile' Mundy's brother's[2] ship, who by the way, I hear is as big a ruffian as ours - or the 'Duke of Wellington'[3]. I am not proud myself, but would much rather go home in one of the transports.

They say that the Russians know everything 15 hours after it has taken place at Paris or London per telegraph.

How jolly it will be when we all meet together again, what a sell if it ends in a campaign in Asia, a beleaguered climate too, to fight in. John's last says that we have no chance of going to India, which is a good thing. I hear that Aldershot is to be the destination of us till the Militia can clear out of Barracks, how odd it will seem returning to

---

[1] A medium-sized duck with a round head and small bill, many of these birds visit the UK in winter from Iceland, Scandinavia and Russia.

[2] The *Nile* was commanded by Captain George Rodney Mundy from 17 July 1854 to 20 April 1857.

[3] Built in 1853, HMS *Duke of Wellington* was the largest ship yet built for the Royal Navy and was the flagship of the Fleet.

civilized life. I expect there will be not a few startled at Crimean heroes expressions and acts at finding home.

Such a sell yesterday in General Orders. No medals to be issued to those who arrived after the 9th September & those who have had them, have to return them. I am sorry for Bayliff who wants one & is most anxious for another campaign with a good many youngsters who have seen no fighting. I think they would be sick of it before it was half over. Muir[1] Surgeon says he thinks both Donovan & Wickham can never re-join on account of their wounds.

Peter is looking to getting a Regiment Majority but unless by Donovan I do not see how he is to square it. Lacy, I doubt purchasing, Ingle cannot ride and would never purchase at rate to stay as major in the Regiment and if Fitz[2] could only get an opportunity of any description, his stay would be short. Poor Peter has been laid up for the last week with a bad attack of rheumatism in his right shoulder and of course confined to house. I had to write an epistle to his governor for him on Tuesday.

I hope by this time or rather long ago, both the Governor's leg is all right and gives him no pain, and that you are quite recovered from the effects of influenza.

I shall expect the Governor, John and Dick to meet me on arriving in England if they can manage it & see the 'two 3s' alias 'the Duke's own' disembark. What fun it would be especially if you could come too. If we disembark at Portsmouth or Plymouth it will be quite handy for Helen and Edward. I am first for leave of the captains & which I shall go in for <u>rather</u>.

---

[1] Surgeon W. M. Muir, MD - 33rd Regiment.
[2] Major H. Fitzgerald - 33rd Regiment - absent wounded 18th November 1854 returned 5th January 1856.

I am sorry to hear that Parsloes is empty still and H & D departure is so near. Will you thank them both for their letter which reached me on Tuesday last, I will write soon. I have not heard from Malta for an age. Eleanor is a bad correspondent and if she wants to hear from me she must answer my last two letters, as one does not come up to my idea of fairness.

Poor Charlie, I hope will be all the better for the sea voyage, it is a melancholy thing. Eleanor, I doubt seeing the Crimea this year, our theatre was a failure, at least we have got none. Tonight I am going to the 7th theatre, a dress rehearsal. Tomorrow I am on the Fort Paul picquet rather a good guard now there is no firing, & a short one. It is light now till 7 o'clock. Today it is awfully cold and looks like snow. I hope it will keep off till after tomorrow night as it will be slightly frigid by the water side. Bayliff is very fresh & well and desires to be remembered to you all, ditto Peter.

I must stop this epistle with best love to you all - tell Dick to write. Is the shave true about the Sultan[1] giving us a medal? Rather a swell with two medals.

Goodbye dearest Mother and believe me to be ever your most affectionate son,

Basil

It is snowing here and regular winter again.

---

[1] Turkish Crimean War Medal issued by Sultan Abdülmecid I of the Ottoman Empire to allied military personnel involved in the Crimean War of 1854–56.

Written by Thomas Basil Fanshawe - to his father, Thomas Lewis Fanshawe.

[Post Script written above the address]
I should like to hear that you had found a tenant for Parsloes and the Docks begun – our mail due yesterday is not arrived yet. We expect news by it of war or peace.

Camp Sebastopol
Good Friday March 21st (1856)

My dearest Gov.

I cannot let this post pass without thanking you for your last & say how sorry I am to find that you have been a prisoner indoors for the last fortnight with your leg but I trust that long since you have quite recovered the use of that limb & are able to walk on the marshes[1] & also into the snipes in the same way too, as in former years. How I wish I was with you to enjoy the shoot.

I enclose this in an epistle to Den in which I have given him an account of my shooting on the Tchernaya on Monday & Tuesday last. Pretty early in the morning I bagged 4½ brace of teal[2], snipe & plover[3] & lost 2½ brace more for most of a day. I shot stunning well & was in camp again before twelve o/c – it is the most lovely ground

---

[1] The marshland situated south of Dagenham village on the northern shore of the Thames estuary had for centuries been valuable pasture land for sheep and cattle, but was subject to frequent flooding. It was an ideal habitat for wildfowl. At the end of the 19th Century it became a centre for new industries and shipping situated along the riverside.

[2] Teal are small dabbling ducks showing bright green wing patches in flight. In the UK they breed and gather in low-lying southern and western wetlands but many migrate from the Baltic and Siberia.

[3] Plover is the group name for several wading birds that have short to long legs and short bills and are identified by their characteristic run-stop-tilt forward movements on open ground.

for wild fowls you can imagine. I wish you and I had the exclusive right of shooting, it is such bliss in the river to come on the duck. Fancy my getting a right & left at him in a corner, knocking things over & losing both. Of course, the shooters during the day are nearly as numerous as the ducks but I got down by five o/c & two such startling cold mornings as they were.

The Armistice[1] now notified in General Orders this day week and on Saturday, in fact ever since, the Tchernaya, the left bank of which is our boundary, has been like a fair. Russians on one side & Allies on the other but they are not very particular as to the line of demarcation. Some of them are fine looking men generally clad in their grey great coats & hardly one without a medal, some have a good many too. Their medals and ribbons for Sebastopol[2] is rather a pretty one, alternate stripes of black & yellow the ribbon. They seem well dressed but I fancy only the best Russians were allowed to come down for Monday next.

The Crimean Spring Races[3] come off in the Valley of the Tchernaya, for the Ruskies especial delectation. I wonder if they will be astonished at our performances in the pigskin[4]. I hear that the entries for the different stakes are numerous – 40 horses entered for one race. I know the Russians invited one or two of our fellows 33rd – to go over & shoot saying they had capital shooting - cocks, partridges, hares and <u>foxes</u> and no end of wildfowl. I heard of an English officer killing 7 couple of snipe on the Russian side of the Tchernaya but I hardly think it is worthwhile risking one's commission for a few birds, fond as I am of shooting.

---

[1] Peace negotiations at the Congress of Paris and the signing of the Treaty of Paris, 30th of March 1856.

[2] Russian Imperial Military Medal – Crimean War 1853-1856.

[3] Reported in Illustrated London News – 'The Spring Meeting Before Sebastopol, The First Jump, Second Race'.

[4] 'The Saddle' – pigskin leather for strength and longevity.

The Crimean footraces came off on Wednesday it was a fine day & a man of my company licked the whole army.

There is not a single fort standing on the south side of Sebastopol, all the White Buildings used for barracks are destroyed, except the outer walls to prevent the Russians from being over curious as to our doings. The Redan is being broken up for the wood the bunks were made of & the whole town is a perfect ruin. Wood very hard to get, I was down yesterday working at the destruction of the Redan, and what a blessed cold day it was. North east wind cut one in half and heaps of dust. The ships in harbour appear to me not to be so many across the mouth that is between Fort Paul & Fort Catherine. Perhaps the action of the waters has destroyed them. I do not think it likely they will try the game of blowing them up. I do not see how they will set about it. The Fort Paul picquet is discontinued during the Armistice – much to everyone's satisfaction who had to go on it. I just escaped last Saturday, the order for its being discontinued coming out that night.

I went to the 7th theatricals instead, a far jollier way of passing the evening and I tuned up with harmonies to an advanced period of the night.

I know you hate crossed letters, so with best love to the Missus and yourself, dearest Gov – ever your affectionate son

Basil

Written by Thomas Basil Fanshawe - to his mother.

I am glad to say our hens have taken to laying & as the warm weather increases hope to get a good supply per diem. Peter and Bayliff are flourishing & desire remembrances.

Camp Sebastopol
Monday April 7th (1856)

My dearest Mother

Many thanks for your last of 17th March. I wrote to John this day week. Not my usual day but I was out shooting on the Friday and so I was last. I got 2 couple of snipe on that day & 3 couple on Saturday and a mallard[1]. I am going out again tomorrow if not prevented by duty. Our weather has been very changeable. On Monday it snowed a little, on Tuesday it was a fine warm day & I spent from eight o/c in the morning till five o/c in the afternoon superintending the men at bull firing[2] – a most lively amusement as you may imagine. However with lots of papers which arrived the evening before & beer & sleep, I managed to get through the day in a secure corner. Whilst occupied in this amusement, we heard the salute of 101 - notifying peace was officially announced, and very glad I was to

---

[1] The green glossy head of the male Mallard would have been a familiar sight to TBF on Dagenham Marshes where they enjoyed a perfect winter habitat after migrating south from their cold breeding grounds.

[2] Extract from the new drill published in 'The Infantry Manual containing Directions for the Drill and Instruction of Recruits, the Manual Exercise, the Revised Platoon Exercise, an Abstract of the Field Exercises and Evolutions of the Army &c. &c. &c.' (Whitehall, 1854): *Too much pains cannot be taken to ensure that the soldier takes a deliberate aim at some specified object whenever he brings his firelock to the Present; and if no natural object presents itself for the men to aim at, several small bull's-eyes must be marked on the barrack wall.*

hear it. The shaves that had been flying about were something curious, first peace & then war to the [xxxxx].

The Russians come over to fraternize to an immense extent, we had two Imp. Artillery officers over yesterday in our mess hut, they had lunch – bread & cheese. English draft beer & sherry, all of which they seemed to approve of most highly, if you may judge of the quantity that they drunk. We English are not allowed to cross the Tchenaya yet, the French do & when shooting I saw stacks of the French going into the Russians lines, far in.

I hear that papers are going to be given in a certain proportion to each Division signed by General [Suders] to allow English officers to proceed into the interior. Sebastopol & Bakchi Sarai[1] & the North side will I suppose be the most frequented places. Of course I shall go if I possibly can, no doubt it will be very amusing to see the Russians & their country. I cannot say that I strictly confine myself to this side of the Tchenaya when shooting but as the field officer who has to visit the line of demarcation seldom marks the line till past 1 o/c & I am in camp generally by that time, as mostly I am down by daylight, I don't think I run much risk.

Thursday we had snow about 4 inches deep & sharp frost, ditto without snow on Friday. Saturday, yesterday & today have been lovely unusually spring days, bright hot sunshine & warm south west wind & on Saturday when shooting, all the frogs were chirping in chorus[2], which in America is a sure sign of approaching warm weather.

The shaves now are where the destination of each division is to be. I most sincerely hope that all division brigades will be brought to an

---

[1] 15 miles (approx.) east of Mackenzie's Farm.
[2] A small chorus frog found in Eastern USA & Canada, having a chirping call said to herald the beginning of Spring – commonly called the 'spring peeper'.

end, it will be rather too much of a good thing if we have to teach Regts who have seen no service lately, how to pitch tents etc. They will have their optics opened by some Crimean dodges, if they have not been already, by fellows who have gone home on leave. The prevalent shave is that the French are to go home at once, then the Sardinians, stores (luggage), Land Transport Corps, Artillery & then the Army. Report says that a division is to be formed of those Regts who have been the shortest time out here, to occupy some part of Turkey for a period. This will not take us of course. General Yorke[1] our Colonel & Military Secretary of the Horse Guards wrote to Mundy short time back & said he expected the Regiment home shortly – no bad authority & I hope he may be correct in his views. There is also a report that the authorities are going to reduce the army by one Lt. Col. (which will be Mundy in our Regt.), 4 Capts, 7 Lts & 7 Ensigns. I don't believe it – it would not make much difference to me if they do or do not, & among the Capts who will be included, there is only one who I should be sorry to see leave.

Will you tell John that I got his last all right & that Bowles[2] of the Berkshire Militia now quarters at Corfu, has been paying a visit to a cousin of his in the Regt. He asked after you all & desires to be remembered. I did not see much of him as he was making the most of his time, which was short, in seeing the different places, but what I did see of him, I liked. He went away on Saturday.

Tell Dick that White 68th has also been up from Malta on leave & Flint of the same Regt. is expected daily. Rogers arrived on Saturday, tell him with whiskers gone & looking more elongated

---

[1] General Sir James Yorke Scarlett, GCB (1799 – 1871) - 5th Dragoon Guards - hero of the Battle of Balaclava – with just 300 Inniskillings and Scots Greys he lead The Charge of the Heavy Brigade. Taken by surprise, the Russians, who greatly outnumbered the British, collapsed their formation and were routed.
[2] Possibly Capt. V. H. Bowles - 63rd Regiment.

than ever. He told me that he had called in sick to ask if he had anything to send out to me but I could not catch him at home.

The mail on Saturday brought me no letters but newspapers. Our mail due today has not arrived & no appearance of it.

The French gave a Ball close to the Sardinians Camp to commemorate the birth of the Imperial Prince[1], to which all English ladies and British officers in the Crimea were invited. I did not go, some of our people went & said it was a decided sell as a Ball, no ladies but vivandières[2] & that style & supper you had to pay for at a most exorbitant price.

What do you think common shot for snipe etc. sells for? 1/6d a lb, a tidy amount for it, but it is that or none.

Theatricals are still being kept up, but the 4th Division do not seem to take as much interest as formerly in acting, at least their performances are not nearly as often as they were. I heard from Malta on Monday last, not much news. Eleanor seems to have given up the idea of coming to the Crimea – lots of Balls going on in Malta.

I am very glad to hear that the Governor suffers no more pain from his leg. I hope he has long ere this escaped from the confinement of the house. I shall be glad to see his handwriting again when he can

---

[1] Napoléon Eugène Louis Jean Joseph Bonaparte, Prince Imperial of France: born 16 March 1856, only child of Emperor Napoleon III of France and his Empress consort Eugénie de Montijo. After his father was dethroned in 1870 the family lived in England where the Prince Imperial trained as a soldier. He served in the British Army in the Anglo-Zulu War during 1879 and was killed in a skirmish with a group of Zulus.

[2] Vivandière - a French name for women attached to military regiments as 'sutlers' or canteen keepers, a function that led to 'cantinière' sometimes being changed for the original 'vivandière'. They were championed by Napoleon III and he doubled their numbers in 1854. They served alongside French units during every campaign of the Second Empire.

find the time. Gaspard was to have started last week for England but they stopped all steamers and transports leaving Balaclava & unless he went by the mail from Kasmisch I do not see how he could get away. I think Billy is quite right to ask for substantive rank as they have given it to several fellows quite as young, Lowbygen for instance, but I should think he would remain (cosy) while on half-pay if he succeeded in obtaining it when peace is signed.

I hope that the docks will take place at once & you will find no more difficulty in getting a tenant for Parsloes. The Denisons have left by this, I suppose – what a change it will be to both you & them. I am sorry to hear the Eagle[1] is departed this life, poor old bird & also his [xxxchand]. I wish Dick was out here now as I have shot two or three birds of the duck tribe & also some waders that I never have seen or heard of before.

We had a salute of 101 guns for the birth of the prince on yesterday week. Remember me to the Bramfields when you see them & all old friends in the village. I have not seen Kettle lately, I told him he could always have the County papers if he liked.

With best love to the Governor & the same to yourself.
Believe me ever dearest Mother, ever you most affectionate son

Basil

---

[1] Dick Fanshawe, TBF's brother also mentions the Eagle in his letters - presumably the Eagle was a family pet, most probably a parrot.

Written by Thomas Basil Fanshawe - to his brother, John Gaspard Fanshawe - copied by their mother.
Camp before Sebastopol
Monday April 14th (1856)

My dearest John

Since my last this day week to my Mother, I have been on fatigue twice, carpeting up shot & shell from the port of the Redan to the Woronzoff road for conveyance to Balaclava.

On Wednesday I went down to the Tchenaya to shoot but there was some rain in the night before which melted the snow on the hills. The valley was full of water, consequently I did no great damage among the birds, only 3 snipe & 1 cockerel - that day permission was given to cross the Tchenaya to go to the Russian side.

On Thursday, I got your letter, many thanks for it. Friday Carr, Vaughan[1] & I started for the Bakhchi Sarai leaving camp about 4 o/c & arriving at Sarai about 10½. It was a lovely day & we had a charming ride, though rather a long one. There and back is about 50 miles, my pony came back very fresh after carrying me well. We went over Traktir Bridge up to McKenzie Heights where the Russians have a scary position & a very scary troop of men. Guns flanking the road on every available place & breach work in the cliff, altogether anything but a pleasant place to go at. Then on to the Balbec, across huge dusty plains with very little water to be obtained, the Balbec is a pretty stream with some wood on its banks, hardly any elsewhere, the Russians having axed it for fires during the winter. About 4 miles beyond the Balbec is the Katcha, much resembling the former river, good wooden bridges across each & large camps at both places. At the Balbec some 10 or 15,000 men, not quite so many at the Katcha. Bakhchi Sarai is about 8 miles from this

---

[1] Lt. G. Vaughan – 33rd Regiment - arrived in Crimea 28th September 1855.

river, it is situate in a valley between two ranges of mountains, almost perpendicular it shoots the lights rays right into the town and it must be a regular oven in summer.

The town itself is like most eastern cities, narrow dirty streets & puts you in mind of Constantinople. There are some decent looking shops for [xxxxx] commodities, but I saw nothing worth bringing away. The only icon is the ancient palace of the Khans of the Crimea[1], it is much the worse for wear & which the Russians have turned into a hospital. I can well imagine it to have been a fine place originally. It is decorated like all eastern swell places, with gold etc., but nothing is done to keep it in repair. There is also a Jewish monastery[2] about 2 miles off, but we heard such conflicting opinion about its being worth seeing, that we did not go to it.

We found very good restaurant in the place & had a capital dinner of cutlets beef steak, the best I have eaten since leaving England, Caviar fresh, a couple of bottles of the wine of the country, something like a light claret, not bad tipple – coffee with fresh milk & cigars. And the damage for the whole <u>three</u>, 27 shillings – not bad!

The town is full of Russian soldiers. Cossacks with their long lances and every other branch of their army. The prettiest dress I saw was an officer of the Hussars or Hulans I think they call them – a green tunic, not very dark, edged around the wrists, skirts & collar with

---

[1] Bakhchisaray Palace - The Khan's Palace or Hansaray located in the town of Bakhchi Sarai - built in the 16th century, it was occupied by a succession of Crimean Khans. The walled enclosure contains a mosque, harem, cemetery, living quarters and gardens.

[2] Chufut-Kale, a medieval city-fortress in the Crimean Mountains, known as Qırq Yer (Place of Forty) and The Rock of the Jews is now a ruin. It remains a national monument of Crimean Karaite culture and is sited just less than 2 miles east of Bakhchi Sarai.

black astracan fur[1], braided across the front something like our rifle tunic, are two gold cords rather like the horse artillery. We fraternized with a Russian officer who spoke French very well. We saw numbers of Russian ladies got up in silks and satins of the best fashions, at least they seemed so to us, but we have not had much opportunity lately of judging of these things.

The Russians have an enormous lot of men in hospital – the officers we spoke to said in summer the dust was nearly a foot deep, consequently mud in winter – pleasing place to live in. We left the place at 2½ o/clock, got to camp at 8 o/clock at night, having had a most satisfactory day.

I get dreadfully tanned & if this hot weather lasts I shall be as black as a bat. The last week we have had lovely weather, but rather too hot. Yesterday I went over to the north side & saw all the forts – Severnya which is a very large one, the Wasp[2] battery which is a very pretty one, a sort of mark tower with a deep ditch & then escarpment with a tremendous earthen embankment, on the top of the tower 8 guns on traversing platforms; everything very clean & in good order. Then to the batteries facing seawards – on to Fort Constantinople which does not seem a bit hurt by our ships fire & Fort St. Michael, just opposite Fort Paul or rather what was that fort, both the two last have numbers of men in them. Most of the men Militia, these are known from the regulars by wearing a cross on their forage caps & allowed to wear beards which the army is not. The casemates in which they live seemed very clean, but very close & fusty.

---

[1] Astrakhan or astrachan is the tightly curled fleece of the fetal or newborn karakul lamb. Astrakhan has a distinctive tight, whorled, loopy surface with a slight sheen and the younger the lamb, the tighter and shinier the loops. The fur comes in a range of shades from pale golden yellow to black.

[2] Fort Wasp - a harbour defence that had 8 large guns mounted on the cliff to the north of Fort Constantine that were able to inflict considerable damage on the British ships when the harbour was bombarded.

I saw Tom Pakenham today going on board ship for England, lucky dog - getting away on leave! No doubt you will see him soon, he has been seedy but looks all right now – getting away from this is as good a cure as anything.
I have been trying hard to get some Russian crosses in silver & brass – at present I have just only 4, I shall endeavour to get more.

The mail today brought no news as to our future destination. The Sardes & French are being packed off by degrees. This week it was our turn: today we had a Brigade field day, awful hot but it was not a very long one. Tonight I am going to dine with the Genl. & go to the Fusilier theatre after. Tickets of each for the benefit of the sufferers at Covent Garden[1]. I mean to get 3 or 4 days leave next week & go up to the Alma, Sempheropol & then home by Yalta & Baidar. If I can manage it I shall have a most pleasant trip, of course I shall give you full particulars.

The Russian soldiers salute you by taking off their caps & holding them till you pass, <u>all</u> salute you, at least they did so to us.

We have very little deer shooting here, but in Asia Minor I believe you may get any amount, wild boars, pheasants & trifles of that sort.

There is not a word of regimental news – Goodbye, love both from your affectionate brother

Basil Fanshawe

---

[1] Theatre Royal, Covent Garden, Drury Lane, London – where a disaster had occurred 5th March 1856 when it was hired for a masked ball by a man known as the 'Wizard of the North'. It was burnt to the ground in a night of drunken revelry and had to be completely rebuilt.

Written by Thomas Basil Fanshawe - to his mother.
Camp Sebastopol
Friday April 25th 1856

My dearest Mother

You must not fancy that because you have not seen my first, the last two mails that it proceeds from laziness, but really because I have nothing to tell you since writing on the 14th to John & then I told him of my day up the country. Lots of our people have been since, no less than 10 are away today on three days leave which generals of divisions are authorised to give - but 7 came back tonight.

This last Thursday, the whole of the British Army in the Crimea were inspected by Codrington with General (Linders). Of course, The Times correspondent has sent a full account so I shall not give you one, as his must be necessarily much better than mine as when you are with your regiment you see nothing at all. We did not get back to camp till a ¼ to 8 o/c and as our servants have to go to these parades, one suffers in having to wait a long while for dinner & then most probably get a very indifferent one.

We had some races & games for the men of the regiment the day before which served to disturb the monotony of camp life, but except that, I have been doing nothing except carry that infernal shot which is the stupidest game out. Now they have got a ship close to the shore in the docks at Sebastopol, so we do not have to carry quite so far. I wish it was over!

On Monday last we heard that 9th, 17th, 62nd & 63rd Regiments are under orders for Canada. They may consider themselves fortunate in having such a good quarter. Yesterday I heard a shave that 30 regiments are to go to England, 17 to the Mediterranean & the 4 which are for Canada will just clear the whole army out of the

Crimea & how soon I care not. Also another shave floating yesterday that the Guards & Light Division were the first to move after the Canada Regts. Yesterday, Codrington had the whole six divisions of infantry out again on Balaclava Plain, we advanced in two lines which extended from one end of the plain to the other. He then rode down the lines with some swell in the shape of a Russian Prince, name I heard but could not pronounce it, much less spell it. We had two Russian officers staying with Mundy the day before the review last week, one the Colonel of a Militia regt, the other an officer of the 6th Hussars his A.D.C. The Colonel only spoke French but his A.D.C. English very well & French.

I hear the Russians were very much astonished at our appearance & particularly our Artillery. They would hardly believe that the horses had been out the whole winter. The French had been reviewed in the morning, so they had an opportunity of comparing the two armies.

Our weather has been warm but not agreeable in consequence of the very cold winds. Yesterday and today are very pleasant, no wind just hot & one can bask in the sun quite comfortably. Mundy just now is in a peak state of mind, as we expect that rip[1] Johnstone to come out and take the Regiment home. He had much better stay at home, as he has shirked the whole time, not having been out 4 months since March '54.

I saw Kettle last week who told me he expects to leave for England this week & offered to take anything home for me. I have got nearly 18 brass crosses from the Russians, a couple of little gold ones & medallions, but I shall keep them till I bring them myself. The gold ones were brought by one of our fellows from Sempheropol. I don't think I shall go there as I hear it is cleared of interest. I shall go to the Alma & if possible to Yalta by Baidar and the Phocas Trap but not

---

[1] Slang for a cheat, swindle, or theft – (modern form – a rip off).

before the trees begin to look green. I have done nothing in the shooting line lately, but mean to turn my attention to fishing in the Tchernaya. I hear there are chub which weigh from two to 7 & 9 lbs each – it will be something to do.

I heard on Monday from you & yesterday from John & Helen. Tell John that till yesterday I had not heard from him for over a month. Our mails have come in most regularly on the Monday & Thursday lately.

I hope the children have all got over the Scarletina[1], what a lucky escape Charlie had in not hurting himself when he fell. I am very glad to hear that the Gov's leg is so far progressing as to be able to move about & also that the warm weather has driven away your cold and influenza. Helen in her letters, I am sorry to find does not mention anyone having taken Parsloes. I should be so glad to hear you at last succeed in getting a tenant for the place – what a shame that Miss Fanshawe has not returned the family plate. John I am glad to hear, gives better accounts of Charles Gostling.

I heard from Eleanor on Monday week last and she informed me that the Col. and herself were coming up to Sebastopol. Myself, I think a camp life rather unfit for ladies, but that is her own look out. The General, when I told him said he would give them tents if they came & I suppose they will live with him. Mrs Strau has been very seedy lately, rheumatism I believe. Eleanor must look sharp or we shall be out of this. All our youngsters are in a poor state of mind at the thoughts of being removed, especially if they are turned loose with only a year's pay, as none of them have served long enough to

---

[1] Scarlatina (or Scarlet Fever), an airborne infection mostly affecting children with symptoms of a sore throat, fever and a characteristic red rash. The possibility of serious complications was a great concern as the illness could lead to heart valve disease and even death. Now known to be caused by bacteria, this illness is today relatively uncommon and easily treated by antibiotics.

permanent half pay. Bayliff I am sure will hardly escape being in the break. I wish it was left to the officers commanding & some 3 or 4 officers in the Regiment to decide who should go. We might be able to make a very decent weeding & very satisfactory to everyone, except those perhaps who were not to remain.

I saw Milly Tupper on Sunday very fresh. He walked part of the way with me to Balaclava where I was going to dine & sleep on board the 'Gibraltar' which ship brought me out from Cork to Malta.

Thank John for the air pillow & stuff for mending waterproof which I got last Saturday from Connell. Dick's pipe for Tillbrook 50th Regt. has never turned up yet. I suppose it will someday or other. Thank Helen & John for their last letters, I won't promise to write next mail as I may not have anything to say but I will write soon. Blank by now Dick for me, he has never answered my last about 5 months old now. Remember me to the enquiring friends and with best love to the Gov & yourself,

Believe me ever dearest Mother your most affectionate son

Basil

I know this is an awful stupid letter but I cannot help it – there is nothing stirring.

Written by Thomas Basil Fanshawe - to his mother.
Camp Sebastopol
Thursday May 15th 1856

My Dearest Mother

Yesterday's mail brought me your last of 28th April. I was sorry to find that the Governor had been laid up with fever. I trust by this he is quite himself again and I shall see him & all of you shortly in a flourishing condition. What a jolly meeting we shall have!

I wrote to John about a fortnight back & had I had anything to tell you should I have written last week, but nothing is stirring & this I am afraid you will find stupid in the extreme. The mail due today brought me a line from John saying Bab was improving and is now I presume stopping with you.

Many thanks for the 'Illustrated News', one of which I got yesterday & one today. They will be highly appreciated in the company.

Tomorrow I am going to Alma with Collings and Muir. Our day starts about 8 o/c, sleep out on the river taking a tent and all things needful with us & return the next day. I have not been anywhere but Bakchi Sarai except yesterday when I went with about a dozen fellows, mostly 68th men, up to a village to the left of Tchernaya called Tchonguna. A very pretty place, some very fine walnut trees & lots of fruit trees, in fact a regular orchard with a little brook running through it. We were to have had lunch there but a beastly French picquet would not allow the cart containing the eatables to cross the Tchernaya without a pass, so we had to ride back & had dinner on the banks of the river by Tchonguna at 5½ o/c - & a capital lunch it was. We wound up that evening at the 68th mess where I met

Master Milly Tupper, who was asked to dine with Jonny Seymour[1] but the last was with our party.

I am thinking of going about the end of next week with Collings to Yalta which is the only part of the Crimea worth seeing. This trip will take about 5 days to do it comfortably.

Cricket is the rage now. Monday & Sunday last the Guards played with an eleven called the Leg of Mutton Club & got licked by eight wickets. If this match appears in Bell's Life ask Edward if he takes that paper, to send it to me - one of our fellows was in the eleven & kept wicket capitally. One day last week we played the 7th & licked them easily, today the 33rd officers played 15 of the men & we only just managed to beat them.

On Saturday we were inspected as a division down in the plain by Sir Wm Codrington, it was very hot & dirty & I rather enjoyed the pull I had of being mounted as acting Major.

Tell Dick, Captain Read & Mrs Glover of the 'Antelope'[2] came up to camp last Saturday week & I went & dined on board the following day. Mrs Read is not on board, but Mrs Glover is and Glover has engaged to take horses to England for about £20 each, to Malta 12/-. I should like to get my pony home free which I may just possibly have the luck to do - he is in tip-top condition.

We are still without official intelligence as to the Regt's destination, but everyone thinks there is no doubt about the old Light Division coming home & the latest shave is that the Guards & Light are to go home at once, to be present at the review of Crimean troops. There

---

[1] TBF family name for Seymour Le Marchant.
[2] *Antelope* - iron auxiliary screw steamer of 600 ton, built at Liverpool in 1846. Purchased in 1852 by a Liverpool Partnership to expand Australian Gold Rush trade, she made her first return voyage to Melbourne in 1853.

was a shave flying that the 33rd was for Corfu – not a bad quarter but England much superior. I heard today that the 34th, 90th, 97th & 82nd Regts were to be the last to leave the Crimea. Except the Canada troops, none have left the Army & we expect to be at least a month or six weeks yet. Our Brigadier told me a short time back that he would have offered to take me on his staff as A.D.C., his former A.D.C. (his brother[1]) having to join his Regt. gone to Canada, but on looking at the state he discovered that we had 5 Captains already on the staff therefore it was no use asking. It might have led to something had I been fortunate enough to get it. He was going to buy my pony for Mrs (Strau) but found that the saddle did not fit him. Mrs S saw the pony on the division field day & said she liked him very much. I could have got from the General £15 - what I gave for him.

I went to the 7th theatricals on Friday last, both pieces I had seen before but it helps to pass the evening. I also went on Tuesday last to see the Sergeants of the 7th act a thundering long tragedy & a stupid farce, incommodious slow, I was glad when it was over.

Our weather has been pretty fine, this morning it rained very heavy but it cleared up at 12 o/c & has been a beautiful day. The country is looking green, particularly the valley of the Tchernaya & away from camp.

The French are embarking rapidly & I heard the last of the Sardes went on board yesterday, so we may begin to move our own men next.

John seems to have been one of the lucky ones at the naval review & to have enjoyed himself very much, more than a good many people do. I suppose the Denisons have shaken down into their new abode

---

[1] Capt. B. van Straubenzee, Aide de Camp - 9th Regiment – arrived in Crimea 9th December 1855.

& are pretty comfortable. What a pity it is that Parsloes is still without a tenant, I should be so glad to hear that you had let it to a pleasant party.

Will you be kind enough to inform me if Dick has been deformed of the use of his arm (right), as I have never had an answer to a letter I wrote him about 6 months back? I shall not bring his stick from the Shadow of Death Valley.

We are busy with ball practice again – the men have to fire 50 rounds away. I have only got through 20 yet. We are also putting up gravestones to the officers and men of the Regt. who have fallen this war[1]. It is a long job as masons are anything but plentiful but I hope we shall do it before we go.

I have heard nothing from Eleanor lately so I suppose they have given up the idea of coming to the Crimea. I suppose Aunt Mary is in England before this. I should think getting away from boiling Malta during the summer would be a great relief to her. How glad they would be to hear of Delancy[2] having passed his examination.

I must say stop – with the best love to the Governor & the same to yourself and all at the Vicarage.

Believe me ever dearest Mother, ever your most affectionate son

Basil

---

[1] The British left behind a number graveyards that marked their camps during the Siege of Sebastopol. All ranks, wives and support staff were buried together. In 1884 with the enlargement of the town it was found impossible to maintain several small cemeteries and the surviving headstones were moved to a single British cemetery at Cathcart's Hill.
[2] Carey Delancy Gostling – 1st cousin of TBF & son of Mary & Colonel Gostling – later of the British Army in India.

Written by Thomas Basil Fanshawe - to his brother-in-law, Edward
Denison - copied by TBF's mother.
Camp before Sebastopol
May 23rd 1856

My Dear Den

I suppose by this time you have quite established yourself in your
new abode and have got things pretty comfortable. I have but little
to tell you, this place is dull from the daily existence – but Friday last
I went to the Alma where the fight took place, it's a pleasant ride of
about 22 miles but with the exception of the valley of the Belbeck &
Kolsha no very great amount of pretty scenery. There valleys are
very pretty, after you cross the last river you have an immense plain
for about 10 miles to the Alma, nothing but grass and rather coarse.
We saw lots of foxes, some partridges & bustards on this plain. The
Alma is a small river you could cross it without getting wet above
your knees in most places. There are one or two deep holes in which
we had a jolly dip on Saturday before breakfast – except the graves,
there is scarcely anything to show what an awful struggle had taken
place there[1]. There are the remains of the Russian redoubt about 100
paces from the river, this is the one so fatal to our regt. It is a much
stronger place than I thought it was from previous description. I
imagine a gentle slope about ½ or ¾ of a mile to the river, with no
end of guns on the crest of the hills blazing at you while going up &
the guns laid to an inch. There are 2 or 3 crosses over some of the
graves, and a grave stone or rather a wooden one over our Regt.

---

[1] At the Battle of Alma the 33rd of the Light Division commanded by Sir George
Brown advanced up the slope towards the Russian positions. Losing its formation,
the British army became a mass of soldiers charging into the Russian troops as they
came down the slope to meet them. Halting, the British fired and caused heavy
damage to the Russian army, forcing them to retreat but regrouping the British
carried on up the slope towards the Great Redoubt. The men of the 33rd were the
first to attack and in the violent hand to hand combat, there were casualties of 7
officers and 232 men.

Grave with the inscription "To the memory of Lt. Du Pre Montagu[e][1] & men of the 33rd Regt. Sept. 1854."

We had lovely weather both days & got into camp just before it began to rain. Monday & Tuesday were both bad days, rain & wind. On Thursday I rode to Kogatch Bay with Collings to see poor Donovan's remains, he was killed on the 8th Sept & put on board ship. The captain of the ship did not half like the job but as he was order by the Admiralty agent to do so, he had no help.

I did intend seeing the Southeast coast to Yalta this week but Collings with whom I was going could not get away Mundy being on leave. We however think of starting out on Tuesday next for a week.

Cricket is now the rage. The 1st Brigade Officer Division licked the 2nd Brigade on Monday, yesterday the staff played the army on the ground behind the Governor's camp. Sir W.C. was present & gave a capital lunch to the players & their friends. The match goes on today, it's generally supposed the staff will be beat. Some wag[2], has called the match the Drones against the Worker Bees. The staff of course come under the head of the Drones. I will send you that result before I close as I am going up to meet a man about a cricket match between ourselves & the 21, in which we have a very good chance of being polished off if we play.

The French are nearly all gone & the Sardes want no more transport. The 30th & 55th embarked for Gibraltar about 2 days ago, the 92nd embarked today for Malta. Not a single Regt has left for England. We are amused at finding the papers say that there is to be a general

---

[1] Lt. Francis Du Pre Montagu - 33rd Regiment - aged 20, son of Lord William Montagu, died at the Battle of Alma on 20th September 1854.
[2] a humorous or jocular person - a wit.

review of Crimean troops on the 29th May[1], considering that except some Artillery and Cavalry who may just reach home in time, not one Crimean Regt. is likely to be in England before the end of July.

General Windham[2] told me yesterday that after the Mediterranean Regt., the Guards & Rifle Brigade start, & that we follow next. But as the Mediterranean stations take nearly the whole of the other divisions eg. 3.4.2. I doubt how we can hopefully proceed for another 6 weeks. Windham said he thought we should get out of this about the end of June, so I suppose about September we have a chance of meeting again.

You must come & see us land, if not disembark, anyway landing. We are getting up a Division lottery for the decks - 217 subscribers at a monarch[3] each. I shall have a try at it – but do not expect to pull any of the prizes! 1st prize £150, 2nd 50 3rd 15, the first would be worth having.

---

[1] Queen Victoria's Journals (Royal Archives) confirm that she reviewed the troops at Aldershot on Monday 7th July 1856.

[2] Lt. Gen. Sir Charles Ash Windham (1810–1870) arrived Crimea September 1854 - appointed Asst. Q.M General to 4th Division, distinguished himself in all major battles and was selected to lead the 2nd Division assault on the Redan in Sept. 1855. Although not successful in taking the Redan, his bravery was praised by Simpson, Commander in Crimea and via reports in The Times his reputation was deemed heroic. In October 1855, promoted to major-general, immediately after the Fall of Sebastopol he took command of the British sector of the city, command of 4th division and at the time of this conversation with TBF, he was Chief of Staff to Sir William Codrington.

[3] A gold coin worth £1 called a 'Sovereign'.

There is not much going on in the racing line, there was some on Friday on the Tchernaya but I was at Alma. I hear a Land Transport man who was riding was pitched off & nearly killed. Young Knox[1] of the Guards I saw yesterday. He is getting over his fall all right. I hope we shall be out of this before the hot weather begins, which is about the middle of June. The weather yesterday already is lovely if it was not for the wind which blows the dust about too much.

I hear that we are to keep the Queen's birthday tomorrow[2], fire blank cartridge & that the French medals in the proportion of 10 to every 100 men are to be distributed. I do not think any of my men will get one. After the liberal distribution of medals from our country, I think this is a shabby allowance.

I saw Mill Tupper yesterday, very fresh & flourishing. Bayliff is well, I fear he will hardly escape the reduction, he will be a great loss to us, but if he is put on half pay I hope it will not be long before he comes in again.

The staff got polished off today, very easy by 70 runs.

The 89 & 13 Regt I hear go on board tomorrow for their destination, the 21st on Monday, they have the pleasant prospect of going into huts at Gozo Malta.

I must conclude this stupid epistle, no doubt much [xxxxx xxxx].
With love to Helen & all friends, I am ever dear Den, your affectionate Basil

---

[1] Most probably Sergeant John Simpson Knox (Scots Fusilier Guards) who volunteered for the ladder party at the Attack on the Redan on 18th June 1855 where losing an arm by cannon shot, he was not deterred and bravely fought on until wounded again. For his valour, the French made him a Chevalier of the <u>Légion d'honneur</u> and later he became one of the first recipients of the Victoria Cross when it was created by Royal Warrant on 29th January 1856.
[2] 24th May 1819.

Written by Thomas Basil Fanshawe - to his mother.
H.M.S London
Sunday 22 June 1856

My Dearest Mother

I send you a line just to let you know how we are getting on, we are about 70 miles from Malta & expect to arrive there during the night: and as it is very uncertain how long we remain there I cannot take the risk of losing the post. We got moved to Kogatch about 12 o/c from our camp, yesterday week & got on board the London[1] with very little trouble. The first night, about 36 of us had to sleep in the cockpit & flaging hot it was. I could hardly get an hours sleep the whole night but the next day Collings offered to take me into his cabin at which I at once accepted & have been very comfortable ever since. It is a part of Capt. Jervis's[2] cabin who commands the ship, a jolly good natured old fellow who does all he can to make the officers comfortable. Half of us mess in the Ward Room & the juniors in the gun room. They feed us very well and in fact we are much more pleasantly situated than we anticipated.

We have had a most lovely passage so far and charming weather, we got to Constantinople on Monday evening & sailed on the Tuesday afternoon about 5 o/c. The morning I passed with the Captain, Mundy & Collings in going over the Mosque of Sultan Achmet[3] & St Sophia, the last I had seen before. Constantinople appeared a good deal changed for the better, the shops much

---

[1] A wooden hulled sailing ship launched from Chatham Dockyard 1840. Commanded by Captain George R Mundy ('Mundy's brother') from 1851 as the flagship of Vice-Admiral Percy. Having spent time in the Baltic and Mediterranean during the Crimean war, Captain W H Jervis took command from early 1856 when as a transporter it brought troops back from Crimea.

[2] William Henry Jervis R.N. aged 53 at this time.

[3] The Sultan Achmet Mosque built 1609 -1616, more known to foreign visitors as 'the Blue Mosque'.

improved & the streets did not stink half as much as usual. Of course, we passed an hour or so in the Bazaar.

We expect to be at Malta 12 hours & then Gib[1] is our next resting place & I hope if lucky in the wind, we may reach home (Portsmouth) about the middle of July. At Constantinople I got your letter dated the 2nd of June & was glad to find the Governor able to use his leg again. I hope it has quite got sound by now. How glad I shall be to see you both again. I was quite surprised and sorry to hear of the Tuppers bad luck, you were the first to communicate it to me; it must have been a heavy shock to them.

I suppose tomorrow I shall meet a lot of old friends at Malta and there are eleven Regts from the Crimean. How glad we all were to leave the place – I fancy by this time, almost all the troops will be out of it as the ships have been passing us in heaps on their way up. To the exception of a man overboard the night before last & who we fished up again, we have had no excitement. On board, the officers of the ship are very nice people and pull with us completely. I have nothing more to add but shall leave this open until I see the Gostlings, if they are at Malta. At any rate, you will know that we have reached Malta all serene, Monday afternoon.

We got in here this morning about 6 & I have found Eleanor and the Col. just going off to [xxxxxx] for a [xxxx]. The latest we sail tomorrow early, it is thundering hot here & the glare hurts my eyes. Goodbye for the present with best love to the Gov. & yourself,
Ever your most affectionate son

Basil

P.S. I suppose we shall be at Gib in a week and then Portsmouth in a fortnight.

---

[1] Gibraltar

The Letters from the Crimea

Written by Richard (Dick) Fanshawe

September - November 1855

Written by Richard (Dick) Fanshawe - to his mother.
Thursday 13 September (1855)
Malta

I will write at once from Constantinople which I expect will be about four days from this. We leave thus this afternoon. I should not be surprised if we stop a week at Constantinople as we have too much cargo to discharge.

My dear Mother,

We arrived here last night at about one o'clock having had a very jolly passage from Gibraltar. I went up to see the Gostlings and dined and slept there. I thought Aunt Mary looking uncommonly seedy, very old and worn and no colour. The Colonel looks as fierce as a pole cat and in great force. Only fancy my disgust at finding that Sammy[1] only left this in the 'Columbo' on Tuesday evening & that I missed him by less than twenty four hours. They seem to think him a great deal better but I don't think from what they say that it will be at all improbable that he will come back to England again before Xmas, as I should say the work is too much for him.

I took a drive with Aunt Mary last night for about four or five miles out of the town. The heat was intense, not a breath of air, in fact almost suffocating. I should think a blade of grass would be a good thing for sore eyes here as I did not see a vestige of one in the place. The chief productions of the place as far as I could see were gnats, dust and prickly pears[2], in fact if any one wished to get himself into

---

[1] Presumably this was Dick's nickname for his brother TBF.
[2] 'Opuntia' the cactus called 'prickly pears' are native only to the Americas. After being introduced into Australia where they were discovered in a farmer's garden in 1839, they then were 'found' in the Mediterranean countries of Africa and arid

good training for the infernal regions I should recommend him to come to Malta, by all means. In my opinion Gibraltar is a Paradise to it.

Aunt Mary seemed very much pleased with the dress but thought it too thick for this weather, so you may fancy how it is.

I have not called at the Post Office yet but mean to do so and leave this letter there. I expect to find one from the Govr giving me an account of the first I wrote to you from the towns and also from Gibraltar. I have not given you an account of St. John's Church[1] as I know you have heard about it very often before. I will only say that I think it one of the handsomest I have ever seen in my very small experience. The gold and paint all very much tarnished which allows ones eye to take in all the mosaic flooring and adds very much to the effect. We were lucky enough to find all the matting taken up so that we saw all the mosaic pave slabs in perfection.

Eleanor has not yet come back and they don't seem to expect her much before November. I saw Geraldine and certainly don't think her a beauty, whatever anyone else may. She seems very delicate.

I have just heard about the Mamelon being blown up by the Russians, it seems to have been gross negligence on the part of the French not to have altered the entrance to the opposite side of the magazine as in that case, of course, the accident could not have happened.

Goodbye with best love to all,

---

southern European regions particularly Malta, where they grow all over the islands. The fruit is edible but must be carefully peeled to remove the small spines on the outer skin.
[1] The cathedral in Valetta, built by the Knights of Malta between 1573 and 1578.

Your affectionate son

Dick

Since I last wrote everyone was obliged to give in and could not face dinner except myself, one passenger and the ship's officers.

Written by Dick Fanshawe - to his sister-in-law, Barbara – wife of his brother John Gaspard Fanshawe.
Saturday 20 October (1855)
Sebastopol

My dear Bab,

I recollect promising to write to you & I am now going to fulfil my promise, although I am afraid that you will not find my epistle easy to read or entertaining.

We expect an attack every day, the whole of the Light Division parade every morning before sunrise that is at a little before five, & think themselves lucky if they get back to bed by six – they carry biscuit & water & in fact are all ready for work. It is expected to come off on Sunday, as the principle they seem to go on is 'the better day, the better deed', of course, no one can tell but the general opinion is that there will be a great battle within the next few days & after that the Russians will evacuate the north side.

We went all over the South side the other day & it was the most wonderful sight I have ever beheld – to see the way in which the place was fortified both as to the extent of the works & the number of guns. I got a little trophy for going, in the shape of a gold locket with a small figure of the Virgin and Child inside which was taken out of Sebastopol on 9th September. The people here are very savage with Genl. Windham as they say he & Russell (The Times Correspondent) dined together the night before Russell wrote his account of the taking of Sebastopol & that he then gave Russell <u>his</u> account of his own exploits, which certainly seem very like the truth as who but himself could have given such an accurate account of them. If such is the case it does not speak much for his modesty.

Sammy and I dined with Tom Pakenham of the 30th a few nights ago, he has been very seedy from a carbuncle in his back which he had neglected, in fact the doctors say that if he had not had it opened when he did it would have gone very hard with him.

Yesterday morning the Russians fired a ground shot from Inkerman which came right through the mess tent of the 34th which is close to this, luckily it was early in the morning & no harm was done. Billy Tupper has got sent home as he is a supernumerary captain, most likely will get about six months leave of absence on arrival – he is looking as fresh as possible & says he never felt better in his life – just the same as Sammy says & looks. I have not seen Milly Tupper since I arrived but shall see him soon.

I like camp life very much indeed but suppose I shall have to leave before long to get back to my work[1] in time, which is the 30th of November, but I think it possible that I shall not be at home at that date as I have made arrangements with another man to do my work if I do not come to time. There is so much to see & to interest one it makes one unwilling to leave sooner than quite necessary. We do not often go down to Sebastopol now as the Russians are always firing thirteen inch shell into it, which makes it unpleasant to ride about as they burst close to you when you least expect it. I was in the White works a few days ago watching the Russians across the harbour, when I heard a bullet shuttle close past my ear from our side, which rather surprised me. Then I saw a Frenchman stand up and pick up a lark in great glee just over my head on the gabions[2] which fully accounted for it – you see them go out lark shooting here with ball cartridges – rather a dangerous amusement for people not engaged in the sport, as they don't care where they shoot & the bullets glance about a good deal in this strong ground.

---

[1] Clerk in the House of Commons.
[2] A retaining wall made of stacked stone-filled gabions tied together with wire - these walls are usually battered (angled back towards the slope).

I paid for my curiosity in going into the underground barracks at the Redan, as I found myself covered in fleas on lying in at night at a grand battue[1] - I had in the blanket next morning I hazard about 15 brace. The other night, Sammy went down to Fort Port on picquet & coming up in the morning was obliged to take off his clothes before he went into his tent & get himself groomed down by his servant, all in consequence of the fleas. Luckily they do not bite me so I do not much care.

I got some amber for you at Stamboul[2] which I hope you will like. I think it pretty, it is lemon colour, the beads that long shape which you so much approved - they are not that clear glass colour but clouded which is the correct thing out here.

I saw a great many Turkish ladies who are pretty in a few cases, very ugly in general. I like their dress very much, except about the feet which they enclose (~~in very loose yellow slippers over~~) in very loose short yellow Wellington boots & put a pair of yellow slippers over them, so they shuffle along in a most inelegant manner as you may suppose. I went on one occasion to see the dancing Dervishes[3] in a mosque at Pera – there were about 20 of them who were walking around a sort of circus boarded all over, they continued this for some time, when they suddenly stripped for action & commenced turning around slowly, they looked over their left shoulder holding their arms extended, the palms of the right hand being held open & forward & the left down. The pace then increased in time to sama music (as they called it) which was like a very bad bagpipe played by a man who had never had one in his ~~(life)~~ hands

---

[1] A hunt that involves the beating of woods and bushes to flush out game.

[2] Another name for Istanbul or Constantinople.

[3] Whirling Dervish - members of the Mevlevi Order of dervishes from Turkey founded in the name of Jalal ad-Din Muhammad Balkhi-Rumi, a Muslim poet and theologian. Rumi taught that followers of Islam could achieve dhikr, meaning remembrance of God, through the use of music, poetry, and dance. The ritual of the whirling dance is called the Sama.

before. This game was carried on for about ten minutes when I left. The howling Dervishes make a great deal of noise & carry on really the same game.

I also went to a Turkish bath[1] where I got all the outside skin taken off me & felt uncomfortable for some days after it.

The Bazaars are the most delightful things possible. I am sure you would spend many days & much money in them with satisfaction to yourself, if not to John. You see the most extraordinary things in the way of amber, slippers, tableclothes covered with embroidery, handkerchiefs, turban cloths, sashes & I know not how many other things which are most enticing to look at. You may sit & smoke there, by the river & the men are only too glad to pull all the things down for you to look at, in fact just the place to suit you, smoking excepted.

It is a very difficult thing to get any Russian booty here now, as almost everything has been bought up but I have got several men on the lookout for me & I am in hopes of adding to my den on my arrival in England.

Fancy the other day when I was in Sebastopol on looking into my rucsac I found a bit of paper which you gave me containing a lock of little Evelyn's hair. I mean to preserve it most carefully & give it you back again in exchange for another piece which has not travelled so far. I expect to find the boy very fresh, able to talk & walk about in great agility – I was very sorry to hear the other day, my Father had been so much hurt on landing in Guernsey, it was very fortunate it was no worse. I hope to find him with my Mother & all of you looking for me on my arrival – I only wish I could bring Sammy

---

[1] Turkish Baths became very fashionable in Victorian England, the first being opened in 1861 – no doubt the enjoyable experiences of other soldiers in Crimea helped to make them popular.

with me for our next Xmas morning. Give my love & Sammy's to John & all at home.

Your affectionate brother

Dick

Don't forget the rabbit who I hope has preserved his accustomed health & vigour – would not give much for his life if he was out here

Written by Dick Fanshawe - to his mother.
Monday 29 October (Sebastopol)

[Note written across the top space – presumably the continuance of the post script –here in full]

You can tell Aunt Caroline[1] that Milly says her spouts of camphor is all rot. I have not opened the quinine cholera medicine[2] or any other of the good things which I brought with me. I hope to deliver them safe into your hands on my return (DV).

My dear Mother

I wrote to the Govr. on the fifth of this month and to Bab on the 19th. I hope they got the letters, we got your last on Saturday as the mail was late. Sammy could not write today as he was on a working party from seven a.m. till five p.m. making roads which as you may suppose is not a very intellectual amusement. The morning parade at five was stopped on Sunday so I suppose there is not much chance of an attack from the Russians for the present. Sammy is not sorry for it as you may suppose as it is very cold at daybreak although the thermometer stood at ninety two in sun yesterday and sixty eight in the shade. I believe it freezes sharp every night. I happen to have only a single tent and in the morning when wake I find the outside of my bed clothes so wet that when I put my hand out it is just as wet as if I had put it in a pail of water, but it make no difference as I find myself as well as ever I was. Fancy my luck in

---

[1] Caroline (Le Marchant) Somerville – Aunt to TBF and Dick Fanshawe, a sister of their mother.

[2] Possibly 'Warburg's Tincture' – widely advertised in 1855 as an *'unfailing remedy in all cases of Intermittent, Continued, Continued-Remitment, Nervous and Typhus Fevers; Cholera, Diarrhoea, and Dysentery; Scrofula in all its forms; Incipient Consumption, Chronic Bronchitic Cough, Want of Appetite, Delirium Tremens, Morbid Digestion, arising from excess in the use of spirituous drinks, Scurvy and every disease of a scorbutic character.'*

weather since I came out. I have been away from England more than two months now and have only had one wet day which was on board ship after we left Constantinople. We have not a drop of rain since I came here except at night.

I have looked for ferns[1] and other plants for you ever since I came out and have not seen one fern except in Asia Minor one day, and they were quite common ones. The only thing in the shape of flowers I have got is some crocus roots which I picked up when they (were) digging the foundations of one of the huts here.

Sammy has not begun his hut yet as he is very busy in making a kitchen and at present there is a great scarcity of men as they are all at work making roads. After all the talk there has been about huts, the officers of this regiment have only one between them which is used as a mess hut. There is no mess at present and I don't see much chance of getting one up as the senior officers don't seem to care much about it. The usual thing here is for two officers to mess together and dine in the mess hut at whatever time they like, which is usually between six and seven. After which everybody smokes and does brandy and water with whist, till about twelve o'clock when we retire to our flea bags and get up to breakfast at about ten, then more smoke and ride. In this way we arrange to pass the time away pleasantly. The huts here are usually dug about four feet into the ground and then a stone wall is built up from the bottom of the excavation to about three feet above the ground. The roof is then put on and forms a very strong building, if it don't leak. I heard here that the new huts they have sent out are a failure as the boards are

---

[1] Collecting ferns was a craze that gripped all levels of society in England from the middle of the 1830s. Books were published to add identification, albums produced for pressing and keeping dried collections and the special indoor Wardian case, a forerunner of the terrarium, helped protect collections from the air pollution of the era.

so thin that you can almost poke your finger thro' them and although they are double they don't keep the wind out a bit.

Many of the officers who I have spoken to still think that the Russians are retreating but of course we should not see it here till the very last, as they would be sure to leave Sebastopol the last, so as to cover their retreat. I think the same myself and we shall see who is right.

We rode over yesterday to the Monastery[1] about seven miles from here it is on the Black Sea about halfway between Balaclava and Kamiesh situated on the heights above a beautiful little bay. We saw service performed by the monks who dress in long black cloaks with round stiff square topped caps from which hangs a black crepe veil which thrown over the back. They wear their hair very long, evidently it is never cut as in some of them it hangs down to their waists, beards and moustache also very voluminous. There were a good many pictures of saints about, whose favourite costume seems to consist of top boots and breeches, with long coats (in latest fashion) of scarlet or blue. The music was very fair and the monks very fat and dirty (I caught lots of fleas on my way back).

The church very small and rickety with a picture of Saint George and the Dragon in brass in a very prominent position, close by a large hole in a door thro' which you looked into an inner compartment which seemed to have also a lot of bad pictures in it. There was another place besides there which was locked evidently not to be seen by the eyes of an unbeliever as I found the keyhole carefully stopped up thro' which I attempted to look. There is a famous spring of water also which we found very good (mixed with some whiskey out of the three gallon jar).

---

[1] Monastery of St Georgia.

The two Carrs and Milligon[1] of the 39th dined with us the other night, we were all at Crofts together if you recollect. To give you some idea of our mode of feeding here I will tell you what we had for dinner. Soup, turbot (native), ducks, green peas (preserved), curried chicken, plum pudding, pancakes, cheese & for drink beer, sherry, port, brandy and whiskey. Nothing to complain of that, I think.

Milly Tup has dined with us on Saturday and we go to dine with him tonight. We saw Gaspard the other day, they both look very fresh and well. I hear that young Tupper[2] of the 23rd is sure to lose his foot if has not already had it amputated. We have not seen anything of John Delancy's son or of young Neave[3] at present. You should be in the Mess Hut sometimes and hear some of the accounts of narrow escapes that have happened to some of the men it seems wonderful how they ever come out alive. Almost all of them who were engaged on the 18th of June and the eighth of September have got holes in their coats and shirts made by bayonets and bullets. One man who I know, was going along the trenches on the 8th behind another officer when he felt a sudden blow and fell down stunned, on recovering he found himself being carried away on a stretcher, so he sung out "Hulloa, where the devil are you carrying me to?", upon which they told him "Sire, your honour, aint you dead now?" He said he thought not and got some water with which he washed his face when he found he was not wounded so he went back to the trenches and found that the officer who had been walking before

---

[1] Capt. Charles Milligan - 39th Regiment.

[2] Lt. James De Vic Tupper - 23rd Regiment of Foot (Royal Welsh Fusiliers) - wounded in the final attack on the Redan - 8 September 1855 – paternal cousin of 'Billy' and 'Milly' Tupper.

[3] Lt. Kenelm Neave or Lt Wyndham Neave – 71st Highland Light infantry - were sons of Sir Richard Digby Neave of Dagnams Park, Noak Hill, Romford a local family probably in the social circle of the Fanshawe family at Parsloes. Both the officers were later killed in the Indian Mutiny as well as another of their brothers - Edward Neave a colonial administrator serving in India.

him had had half his head carried off by a round shot and that the back half had hit him in the face, stunned him and covered him all over with blood and brains etc. and misled the Irishmen.

A sailor who I heard of was carrying a large bag of wool on his back to one of the batteries but they were surprised by the Russians and had to run for it. The sailor hooked it with the bag of wool still on his back. He heard bullets going thud, thud into it and arriving in the trenches for curiosity he cut the bag open when sixteen Russian rifle bullets were taken out. All which must have gone into him if he had not had the wool with him. I could give you hundreds more of this sort but must keep them till arrive home.

I am much obliged for the muffatees[1] which you mention. I have not got them yet and I suppose Kittle has not arrived. I don't much envy him his job of renovating Sebastopol as the Russians fire into it from the North side very briskly at times. When I was there the other day a shell burst so close to us that we were covered by the dust and smoke and the bits flung all around us in grand style, but if you take the narrow streets and dodge about they have not much chance of hitting you.

Many thanks to the Govr for ordering 'The Illustrated' and 'Punch' for me, which I receive very punctually every Friday.

I am thinking of leaving this by the first vessel I can go by after the beginning of next week.

I don't think I shall stop long at Malta as I have no dress clothes and I don't care about the place although the Gostlings are very kind. I

---

[1] A simple type of mitten - with no fingers or thumbs, just an open-ended tube of knitting with a thumb-hole in the side.

may go to Smyrna[1] or Corfu[2] or in fact anywhere on the Mediterranean before I arrive home. If I find I can't be in London by the last two days of November I shan't hurry myself to get back before Xmas day but the chances are that you will see me the last day or two in November unless something fresh turns up here, which don't seem likely.

I should think the Govr would be quite sad that the bridge is at last contracted for, as his favourite hobby will now be gone. I am afraid he will be obliged to have recourse to the old suspension bridge to the church door. I am truly glad to hear that you are both so well and that you enjoyed your Guernsey trip so much. I wonder whether I shall ever get as far myself. I never had any fancy for the place. I am very glad Alice[3] is coming over in the Spring, I expect it will be great fun. I think by this time you will agree with me that I have written enough rubbish so I will shut up with best love to all from Sammy and myself.

Your affectionate son

Dick

---

[1] Smyrna, an ancient city located strategically on the Aegean coast of Anatolia – the modern city today is known as İzmir.

[2] 2nd largest of the Greek Ionian Islands, Corfu had been under British rule since the Napoleonic Wars Later in 1864 when modern Greece was unified the island was relinquished by the British Empire.

[3] Alice Tupper born 1834, a 1st cousin and sister of Billy & Milly Tupper & daughter of Anna Le Marchant & Daniel Tupper.

Written by Dick Fanshawe - to his mother.

Friday 9 November (1855) – [*town not given but Sebastopol entered on the end of last sheet*]

My dear Mother

I have nothing at all new to tell you as nothing has been going on since I last wrote. Sammy left this morning for the Barrack Guard down in the town and will not return till tomorrow morning at ten, it is not a bad guard but there is very little to do except to watch and see where the Russian shells are going to pitch, which isn't a very lively amusement although they come rather close at times, sometimes in the same house with yourself but no one is ever hurt.

We dined with Milly Tupper the other day, who is looking very well but I fancy he finds it slow work. I have seen Gaspard once for about five minutes and went down to Kadikoi today to try and find him, but did not succeed.

I think the probabilities are that I shall start from about Monday or Tuesday, but I cannot be at all certain. I have got an order to go down by the first opportunity that offers as far as Scutari after which I shall take my passage by one of the Cunard boats which go to Liverpool, calling at Smyrna, Alexandria, perhaps Cairo and the Pyramids and so home. I should like to have a look at Egypt and the old Nile etc. and can do it for thirty pounds in three weeks from Constantinople, which I expect to leave on the 17th and to get home in good time for Xmas. I think it will be very jolly.

I have got all sorts of loot to bring home for men out here, among other things a Russian Bloodhound taken out of Sebastopol. My own loot, I am afraid will be but small and not very valuable, but all the things I bring home shall go down to the Vicarage before I send them to their various destinations.

I went down to Kamiesh last Sunday and dined there with Sammy and some more of the Regt. We got a very fair dinner with champagne, claret and beer for fifteen bob each, which I thought very moderate. I expected to have my eyes gladdened with a great display of female beauty in the shops but I am sorry to say that I found them very much overrated. The only girl I saw with any shadow of beauty was the Vivandière of the Imperial Guard, and she was no great shakes.

We heard today of General Codrington being appointed Chief, which has given universal satisfaction throughout this Division but I am afraid that General Barnard's[1] appointment has not been received as one of the blessings of a merciful Providence.

I saw a great bit of fun in the Redan the other day. The Rifles had the Redan Guard and a French soldier on walking thro' remarked "English no bono", upon which one of the Riflemen asked him to repeat it which the Frenchman did, where upon the Rifleman took my friend by the collar with one hand and having extracted a good stick from one of the gabions he set to work and licked the poor devil till he sang out a very different story when he was released and hooked it as fast as his legs could carry him, followed by shouts of laughter from all present. I did not laugh myself, as you may suppose.

I met a man yesterday who had just come from Kertch – who told me that one of the Turks shot at a woman a few days ago. Of course he was had up to a court martial and sentenced to be flogged, which was carried into effect upon the spot. The other Turks did not

---

[1] Sir Henry William Barnard (1799-1857) served in the first Anglo-Afghan War and was newly promoted to major-general on the outbreak of the Crimean War, where in 1854 he commanded a brigade of the 3rd division. When General James Simpson became chief commander on the death of Lord Raglan, Barnard was appointed his chief of the staff, the position he held at the fall of Sebastopol. Afterwards he commanded the 2nd division of the army in Crimea.

approve of it and when Major Guernsey[1] (who had been sitting as a member) came out of the door a Turkish Major drew his sword and threatened him and a private made a prod at him with his bayonet. Whereupon, Major Guernsey drew his revolver and shot the two men dead on the spot, after which the Turks quietly separated. I should think it would be a good lesson to them. I heard a British ensign of this Regiment ask the other day what was the meaning of "Gaglignani's Messenger"[2] and on being told that it meant 'daily news' he quite believed and went on his way rejoicing. I should not have believed it, if I had not heard it myself.

We have been hard at work getting up a cook house and I think we have succeeded very fairly as we have got a grand fireplace and an oven made out of a preserved potato tin which answers first rate with some sand put into the bottom of it to prevent its burning through. Some of the houses that are being built here are most elaborate structures with all the stones squared up in great style.

I was rather astonished to find on the sixth of the month that the thermometer stood at one hundred and eight in the sun and seventy in the shade. The nights however are becoming uncommonly cold, although we have as yet escaped the rain altogether, I think I shall begin to wear one of the cholera belts you made for me. You may fancy what a stage drunkenness has got to out here when I tell you that two men of this Regt w(h)ere brought into Hospital in such a healthy state one night about a week ago, that one died immediately

---

[1] Most probably Heneage Finch - 6th Earl of Aylesford DL (1824 –1871), styled Lord Guernsey until 1859, was a British peer and politician and a major in the Warwickshire Yeomanry Calvary.

[2] From a weekly 'Repertory of English Literature' started in Paris in 1801 by the Galignani family, on the fall of Napoleon in 1814 progressed into publishing guide-books and eventually 'Galignani's Messenger' quickly developed into a daily paper, that enjoyed a circulation among English residents all over Europe – popular due to the stamp duty and postage rendered on London journals being expensive.

Parsloes Manor from the Gorse Brook

Unknown Artist (after 1867)

Valence House Museum

Dagenham Vicarage (1956)

LBBD Archives - Valence House

Dagenham Parish Church

Matt Benjamin (2015)

Dagenham Breach House, 1790

Joseph W. Furnell (1905–1991)

Valence House Museum

and the other within an hour. The same thing happened on the same night to two men of the 23rd and the one of the 7th.

Since I wrote the above, the mail arrived and with it your letter of the 26th. I am very glad you found my letter in any way interesting as I really did not know that I would write such a thing as an amusing letter.

I will write to Sockett either before I leave this or else some place in the Mediterranean. Sammy wrote to him some time ago and I should think you had got the letter by this time as it enclosed to you. Sammy has just sent me up a lot of Convolvulus Major seeds which he has collected today from the "Karabelnaia" suburbs and which shall be duly delivered to you on my return.

I really hardly think that I shall know the place again when I return, with the bridge[1] and the brick wall round the enlarged churchyard[2]. I should say that they mean business about the docks and I believe Sir John Rennie[3] is a very enterprising man and I fancy <u>"a real Scotchman"</u>. The Punch and Illustrated London News have arrived very regularly ever since I came out, except on one occasion some time ago. I will tell you in my next whether I wish them continued or not as I don't know whether Sammy wants them or not. The County Paper and Times have also come very regularly except today when we have got nothing except Punch and Illustrated.

I was very sorry to hear that John had another carbuncle as I know these are very unpleasant things. Tom Pakenham had a very bad

---

[1] The bridge made access easier from the vicarage directly to the side church door, as used by the Reverend Thomas Lewis Fanshawe.

[2] The churchyard of Dagenham Parish Church was extended during this period, confirmed by the Dagenham Vestry minutes (Valence House Archives & Local Studies Centre). They reveal evidence of an extensive discussion concerning the building of the new brick wall.

[3] See TBF letter dated 1st December 1855.

one out here but is luckily quite fit again. I saw him yesterday. I feel convinced that 'the Reaper' will not disappoint my expectations any more than Mr Halls.

Many thanks for the Govr's kind attentions in having the board put up round the eagle's cage. I forget to tell you that I found verbena's growing wild on the Bosphorus? What the colour of the flowers might have been I can't say as it was long past their time for blooming, but the leaf was just the same as ours. I am very glad to hear that yours have turned out so well this year, I only hope that they will stand the winter well.

I am looking forward with great pleasure to see my bedroom looking clean and in good order (as I am sure you have put it) for I have never seen it in that state yet. I have only slept in ~~two~~ three rooms since I left England, one in Gibraltar, one at Malta and the other at Constantinople, so you may suppose I shall be very glad to return to my own little den and it's jolly feather bed.

You ask me how I like being under fire. I was down in the town a few days ago - going into the Dockyard when as I was riding along one side of a high wall a shell just lobbed over my head and burst on the other side of the wall - another six feet would have done it. I was looking over the Barrack Terrace the other day when a Russian round shot carried itself about eight feet below me in the wall that supported the terrace. But no one ever gets hit now, I am sure I don't know why.

I hope Mr Sockett will not <u>commit the folly of</u> getting married as I had a far better opinion of him. <u>Poor man he will soon repent it</u>!!!!!

With best love to all from both of us, I remain your affectionate son
Dick
Sebastopol

Conclusions

After the fall of Sebastopol the Russians quickly pulled out of the area and threatened by Austria potentially joining the allies, they came to the peace table. The Treaty of Paris was agreed and signed on 30th March 1856 and as we have read, the English troops begun to systematically withdraw.

With the Turks now guaranteed security and the Black Sea and Danube open, the French and English rushed to leave. Their casualties had been great, the French suffering most in the second phase of the war, and the populations of both western powers had little appetite to delay their departure. In Eastern Europe, borders moved, new nations evolved from the peace arrangements and alliances changed. These conclusions would eventually lead to create the powder keg that sixty years later started World War I.

Basil Fanshawe left us without news of his next army posting but from family records we know how his career and life moved on. He was posted to India and later to East Africa, serving during the 1867 conflict in Abyssinia (Ethiopia). His letters home from both locations are held in the archives of the Local Studies Centre at Valence House. Hopefully, they too will soon be ready for publication.

To round things off, we can tell you that Basil married Emily Catherine Gosselin on 8th March 1864. They set up home at Bath in Somerset and had a family of six children. He achieved his promotion and on retirement from the regiment in 1878 he had the rank of full Colonel.

Post Script:

'Is the shave true about the Sultan giving us a medal?' 'Rather a swell with two medals'…

Basil Fanshawe so joyfully anticipated both the Crimean War Medal and 'the Sultan's medal that we naturally assumed he had possession of his campaign medals when he died on 4th May 1905. So it was a strange coincidence that as his letters were being transcribed we discovered a medal dealer on the internet offering his Crimea medal for sale. Now safely back in Dagenham, Basil's medal will be kept with his letters. Would he not say that was a capital idea?

Index of soldiers mentioned in the letters

Valence House is the home of the London Borough of Barking and Dagenham's Museum and Archives & Local Studies Centre. It is a focus for the local community heritage projects in which professional staff encourage enthusiastic volunteers to use their natural talents and learnt skills for mutual benefit.

This publication forms part of the Heritage Lottery funded project "Sebastopol to Dagenham", which also includes an exhibition at Valence House from 30th July to 25th September 2016. The volunteers leading the work on this project were Derek Alexander, Matt Benjamin and Deirdre Marculescu. They were assisted by Rosalind Alexander, Pauline Amos, Ray Amos, Frank Beale, Olive Goodman, Tobi Olowe, Lorna Orr and David Porter.

We extend our grateful thanks to Scott Flaving, Honorary Secretary of the 33rd (Duke of Wellington's) Regiment Museum for his support and interest, and to Rosemary Rogers for sharing her knowledge of Dagenham Parish Church and the life and work of the Reverend Thomas Lewis Fanshawe.